MW01483416

THE DRIVE TO THRIVE

ANTHOLOGY

2ND ANNUAL WUFC WRITING CONTEST
WINNING ENTRIES AND DISTINGUISHED GUESTS

The Drive to Thrive
Anthology of the 2nd Annual WUFC Writing Contest
Winning Entries and Distinguished Guests

Writers Unite to Fight Cancer (WUFC)
Compiled by Margaret L. Turley

ISBN Softbound Print: 978-1-939614-24-7
ISBN E-book: 978-1-939614-25-4
Library of Congress Control Number: 2014901775

Cover art copyright Lukiyanova Natalia/frenta/Shutterstock.com

Published by Perfect Bound Marketing
www.PerfectBoundMarketing.com

Visit Writers Unite to Fight Cancer (WUFC) at: writersunitetofightcancer.org

Dedication

To passionate researchers around the globe who strive to win the war against cancer.

To everyone affected by cancer.

Acknowledgments

Thanks to the following individuals for providing their time and talents:

Editors

Charline Profiri

Cynthia R. Roedig

Ethel Lee Miller

Margaret L. Turley

Pamela R. Goodfellow, Ph.D.

Judges

Anna Arnett

Cindy R. Williams

Connie Flynn

Conrad J. Storad

Ethel Lee Miller

Gloria Bonnell

Pamela R. Goodfellow, Ph.D.

Penny Freeman

We also thank all 2013 WUFC Writing Contest contestants and the guest authors for sharing their works of literature.

Table of Contents

Introduction

By Margaret L. Turley, WUFC Administrator

The Drive to Thrive is manifested even from within the womb as a fetus draws nourishment from its mother. Upon birth the rooting instinct takes over as the infant nuzzles until it finds life giving food. The drive to thrive is the reason for finding cures and what makes people endure extraordinary circumstances with hope for a better future.

In choosing the theme: **The Drive to Thrive** we share examples of thriving throughout life's many challenges, not just existing, merely surviving or capitulating in failure. Exuberance of youth, tenacity in advanced age, resilience in the face of various medical conditions, and the will to excel are manifested in the written words compiled in this anthology.

White Lions Living Symbols of the Power of Charity

Lisa Finder

Speech given at the
WUFC Centennial Cancer Research Fundraiser
February 2, 2012

The life of a man consists not in seeing visions and in dreaming dreams, but in active charity and in willing service.

It is my honor to be here with you at this charity event at the beautiful Arizona Centennial ballroom at the Historic Biltmore.

I would like to seize the opportunity to congratulate us on launching this outstanding fundraising campaign in which many urban organizations are involved. Our donations in this month have amounted to thousands of dollars—the sum that will be transferred to two Arizona research projects. The money will be donated for modern medical testing. Our goal is to decrease the number of cancer deaths in Arizona. To achieve this noble goal, we have organized this charity book signing and charity educational speeches. I am honored to thank all sponsors, organizations and private persons, who care for people in need in Arizona.

When I was six I sat by my maternal Grandma's chair while she suffered slowly in the clutches of lung cancer.

When I was eight years old a good friend of our family and medical doctor was imprisoned for suggesting patients take vitamins for cancer. The same year my brother, David left to attend The School of Natural Healing in the United States.

When I was ten years old I walked every day through apple orchards to my paternal grandmother's house. To me she was the epitome of grace and love and fun. She raised 14 children and survived the wild homesteads of Northern Canada.

One afternoon in her 90th year a man broke into her house while she was home and tried to rob her. She grabbed a kitchen chair, shook it at him, looked him in the eye and said "you should be ashamed of yourself." She proceeded to chase him out of her house. She did the same thing with breast cancer when it came to call…she read every book and every news or magazine article on cancer. She did everything from drinking grape juice to surgery. She raised her chair of determination and defiance against cancer and lived many more happy years.

We are here tonight to raise our chairs against cancer. Gone are the days when doctors were imprisoned for treating cancer with natural and traditional methods. But where do we go from here? We do what is being done at Arizona State University and the University of Arizona. We join as scientists, doctors, teachers, professionals, authors and families to bring treatments out of obscurity and educate the world on the choices they really have.

When I was 12 my older brother was just bringing his company White Lion, an extension of the first herbal supplement manufacturing company in western Canada to the Vancouver stock exchange. Life was good. Suddenly in his forties he was afflicted with kidney cancer and given three months to live. He walked away from all things to say good-bye to the world. White Lion died without him. But he didn't die! He healed his cancer. Now he does research with Bob Waters, Head of Arizona State University's Bio-Design Institute Cancer Research Program.

There are many white lion legends in the world; one is about a unique white lion, Letsatsi, who was born into a pride of normal tawny lions. He escapes death many times. The real white lions became extinct in the wild. Between the years of 1993 and 2006 there were no births at all. 1994 was the year that the last white lion was seen in the wild.... Yet.... In 2003, the Global White Lion Protection Trust (WLT) initiated the first ever reintroduction of white lions to their natural endemic range in South Africa. The long-term objective of the WLT is to restore the natural balance.

When I was 19 I was living in Hawaii enjoying the balance of nature and got the call that my Father had stage-four colon cancer with maybe a year to live. My mother and father lived with me for a year on the beach of Oahu facing a disease that was so far advanced there was no stopping it. I still remember my dad standing on the beach and getting knocked down by a sudden wave...and he sat on the sand laughing. He laughed in the face of all life's challenges even to the end of his life. His life was like a legend to me. Legends and real life white lions can teach us many things. Knowledge and education is the key to bringing treatments out of obscurity into the light of our lives.

Three years ago my mother-in-law was afflicted with breast cancer for the second time. She treated it with all methods at her disposal and beat it. The weakened state of her immune system caused her body to give out this New Year's Eve. I know she wants us to press forward one step at a time to make a cure viable before it hits one of her grandchildren or your grandchildren.

As we meet here today my brother-in-law is in the hospital battling cancer using traditional and naturopathic methods. We all will keep searching for a treatment that will bring him home. Onward we will seek for a rebirth for all our loved ones and perhaps even our own one-day.

As a symbol of the rebirth of the white lions of South Africa I started White Lion Foundation in 2009. Since that time, I have found many good people whose lives consist in seeing visions and in dreaming dreams, and in active charity and in willing service. There is a way to make specific targeted therapies joined with natural and early treatment the way of the future. We may not make lives longer yet—but we can make them the best!

We can cure cancer together because we are working as a team for the good of all. Writers Unite to Fight Cancer has been constantly working on fundraising, all of which is transferred as research aid. Today, we are often constrained to our own affairs. We think of our own future, with hopes of change at this time of recession. The natural supplement world is rapidly growing even during these hard times. Why? We all want a better life and better may not be wealthier but it can mean healthier. Life is so beautiful. God presents us with this gift of life not to suffer from devastating disease but to fight. Our mutual efforts, our support—all this—cancer victims need the most. Together, we will fulfill our duty of cherishing every human life.

A New Word

By Bridgett Crosby

My best friend has cancer. My mother in law has cancer. My neighbor has cancer. My friend has breast cancer. My sister had cancer and my cousin had cancer. My friend's wife just passed away from cancer. I lost my aunt, uncle, grandfather and even my mother to cancer.

I get so tired of hearing the word "cancer." Maybe we should strike it from the dictionary and come up with a new word. We could make up something new so that when people hear that certain word, they don't automatically think that the diagnosis is a death sentence.

We could make up a new word that evokes happiness and joy, because there are people out there who have cancer, who had cancer, who are living, enjoying life, they are beating it, and they refuse to give up. They are survivors. They are thriving, reaching new heights, doing things they never thought they would do.

The new word could be a keyword for survival, for defying the odds, for living life to the fullest regardless of diagnosis. I have lost people I loved to cancer, and the pain was real, and raw and something I will never forget. Those people I loved who I lost are not remembered as victims, nor are they remembered as statistics. They were my loved ones. They had names and faces and smiles and tears. They experienced joy and sadness. They laughed with me, they laughed at me, and they laughed because of me. I tried to be a clown if only to make them smile. Sometimes it worked, sometimes it broke my heart, and I would cry later, at home, all alone where I would distract myself and try to think about my favorite subject, words.

I would rack my brain and try out all sorts of words. Silly, funny sounding words like "poppycock" and "gobbledygook" or "gibberish" and "flibbertigibbety." Imagine the look on your friend's face when you have to share the news about your loved one. "Yes, my sister was diagnosed with 'gobbledygook' today. Oh, you've never heard of that before? You say you don't think that exists?" While silently I will revel and cheer on the inside and scream *Yay! It doesn't exist!* and enjoy the confused look in their eyes instead of that dreaded look of pity.

I can almost hear what people would say when sharing the news, "Did you hear about so and so's 'hugger-mugger'?" instead of using that dreaded "C" word. Maybe someone would use this one, my favorite, "Did you hear her mother has the 'jabberwocky?'" (I always picture the Mad Hatter doing his dance and can't help but smile.)

Perhaps you are sitting in the doctor's office, waiting with dread for "the talk" and then you hear the doctor say, "I'm really sorry, but the tests are positive, you definitely have 'callipygian.'" (Which means, you "have an attractive rear end or nice buns.") That would be so much better and you would leave that appointment feeling really good about yourself.

The power we give to words is overrated, especially the power we give to one…little…six letter word. I don't believe there is a more dreaded word in any language or in all of human existence.

I vote we take our power back! We could create a new word with a definition that imparts hope, love, survival and cure.

Cordelia

By Louise Laughlin

Two month old Cordelia experienced extreme bloating every time she nursed. The discomfort caused to her cry. She struggled to breathe. Cordelia's mother, Corrine, took her to a doctor, who could not identify a problem. He suggested that perhaps she was nursing too long each time.

After days of watching her baby suffer at feeding time, Corrine took her daughter to the emergency room. Concerned staff ordered an MRI to determine the issue.

The MRI uncovered the problem. A doctor escorted Cordelia's parents to a private conference room. They worried that they were about to get bad news. They were right. The doctor's words, "I'm afraid I don't have good news. Your daughter has liver cancer" caused both the frightened parents to experience pounding in their ears from elevated blood pressure.

"How can that be? She's only two months old." Corrine was distraught. "What will happen next?"

The doctor bowed his head for a moment before answering. "We need to perform surgery on Cordelia. We'll open her abdomen with an envelope cut which will allow her liver to expand. That will take the pressure off her diaphragm so she can breathe more easily. Then we'll begin treatments to reduce the size of her liver and to battle the cancer."

With tears streaming down his cheeks, Cordelia's father, Jeremy asked, "When will the treatments begin?"

"Immediately."

As she wept, Jeremy cradled his wife in his arms to comfort her. "We need to be strong for our baby."

What followed was six months of surgeries, chemo, and radiation. In addition to a feeding tube, Cordelia had to have a tracheotomy. The trach silenced her cries and babbles, but didn't prevent her alligator tears which were gut-wrenching to anyone who observed them.

Throughout Cordelia's treatments, her grandfather sent regular text messages to update friends and to ask for prayers for her successful recovery.

Six months later, those prayers were answered. Cordelia was winning her brave battle against cancer. The doctor pronounced her healthy enough to go home providing her parents hired a home nurse to administer medications through her feeding tube and to care for her trach. Finding the right person took a week, but Cordelia was finally able to return home.

She continued to thrive, and three months later was declared cancer free. The day before her first birthday, Cordelia's tracheotomy was removed. It had been ten months since her last verbal communication. Her pent-up silence ended, and she began breaking eardrums of anyone within hearing distance.

Though Cordelia was born with a challenging medical condition, she overcame obstacles with courage and determination unusual for one so young. Her story offers hope to children living with cancer, and to their parents.

Happy Birthday, Cordelia. Thanks to God for answered prayers. Sing to your heart's content.

Mistaken Identity

By Betsy Winterman

I work in a little mom 'n' pop restaurant that specializes in Southern food and Southern hospitality. Daisy Mae's is a local tradition in this expanding city – one of the few places left within the city limits where one can go to get good, old-fashioned soul food, and a waitress to call you "sugar" or "darlin'" and bring you your coffee, tea, or Coke before you even get a chance to sit down.

Our customers are as fiercely loyal as they come. Most come several times a week, and a handful come every single day, rain or shine. I've been working for Miss Meghan and Miss Leslie (sisters who own the restaurant and took over management from their mother some 15 years earlier) for just over five months, and there is one customer, Robert Harkness (everyone calls him Bob) who has literally come in every single day for all of those five plus months. He's never even been late. All the waitresses know that at 10:30 sharp they need to get Bob's coffee ready. He even had a designated booth.

One day at about 10:45, I was walking out of the kitchen with Bob's usual order (two sunny-side up eggs on white toast with a side of bacon) when Meghan, who runs front-of-house, came up to me.

"Desiree, drop that food and your tickets and go on break."

This was like any other day. The 11:00 waitress had shown up (we are encouraged to show up early) and was going to cover for me. I dropped my tickets as ordered. With a smile and extra thick Southern accent I checked to make sure my tables had everything they needed. I went to the cabinets reserved for our use, I grabbed my cell phone and cigarettes and stowed them in my apron pocket as I made my way back through the dining room and out through the kitchen.

Being smack-dab in the middle of a Georgia summer, the heat hit me like a wall, which caused me to pause for a second to adjust. There were two folding chairs out back on either side of the door and a coffee tin for an ash tray. I took the chair next to the air conditioning unit. Not only was it closer to the ash tray, but when the exhaust fan was blowing, it also created a nice breeze. While there was no way to carry on a conversation over the deafening whirr of the unit, it didn't matter today because I was alone.

I got out a cigarette and lit it, took a drag and felt the stresses of the day melt away, if only for 15 minutes. Jazmin and I had had it out today. I had borrowed her toast to give to my customer but forgotten to drop another one. Jazmin had completely overreacted. I mean, come on, it was only toast.

I took out my phone and signed onto Facebook, which completely absorbed my thoughts. When my cigarette burned down to the filter, I tossed it and lit up another one. At some point the exhaust fan turned off, I uselessly fanned myself with my ticket book as I dabbed carefully at the sweat on my face trying not to smear my makeup.

About halfway through my second cigarette the back door swung open. The thing about sitting in the chair by the air conditioning unit is that when the door is opened, it completely hides you from view. If the fan happens to be off, like it was that day, it sets you up to take people by surprise and maybe overhear a few things you shouldn't.

"I can tell she's feeling it more this week than usual. It has been really crazy this week, though," I heard Meghan say from where she'd paused on the other side of the door.

I will freely admit to anyone that I enjoy gossip. If there is a secret to suss out, I am usually the one to do it. And, if this secret had something to do with one of my co-workers, I was that much more motivated to dig up the dirt.

"Even still, considering everything she's going through, I'm amazed she's keeping up the way she is," Leslie replied. "I don't think I would do half so well in her shoes. Her tips yesterday were amazing."

"It really makes you think," Meghan commented. "You hear about cancer all the time, but it's just an idea until it hits someone you know. Then all of a sudden it's real. A disease. It's…cancer."

Cancer…I hadn't been expecting that. I wondered exactly who they were talking about, positively burning with curiosity.

I waited to hear more, but both sisters fell quiet for a moment, then I heard their feet shuffle as they continued through the doorway. As the door started to swing shut, it brought me into view. I scrambled with my phone, which had fallen off of my lap while I had been distracted. I raced to adopt a nonchalant pose, as if I had failed to overhear their riveting conversation. As if.

I couldn't see their reactions to my presence. I knew that was something I should not have overheard, so I decided to just stay quiet and keep my head down until either my break was over or Meghan and Leslie confronted me. They didn't say a word.

I checked my watch knowing I'd already gone over my break by a few minutes, and put the remains of my cigarette in the coffee tin.

I got a pretty good look at Meghan's and Leslie's faces as I squeezed by them. I smiled when I saw the nervous set to their jaws. I could tell they thought that I had most likely heard everything, but they weren't sure enough to call me on it.

Awkward silence was replaced by chaotic racket as I entered the kitchen. I hurried through, trying to weave my way around the cooks as they went about their harried movements.

After I had stashed my things back in the cabinet and washed my hands, I got back into the grind. I placed orders, refilled drinks, made sure my customers had all the sauces they needed (ketchup, hot sauce, pepper sauce, etc.), bussed tables, and in general did my job to the letter.

Meghan had a tendency to take her emotions out on the wait staff. The previous week she had been stressed out because her son was starting high school and wrote three of us up for things like not mopping well enough and writing tickets incorrectly – small things that could easily have been talked out (and would have been at any other time). I didn't need any fallout from today's slip.

We stayed pretty busy the rest of the day, so when three o'clock rolled around (closing time on the weekdays) I was more than happy to start my side work. I even made a point of doing the little things that I would sometimes skip out on when I was in a hurry – things like refilling the salt and pepper shakers or combining the Texas Petes. A couple of the waitresses were real sticklers for that kind of thing, but I didn't see that it hurt anything as long as I got to it every couple of days.

It wasn't until I started rolling silverware that I had a chance to think over what I'd heard (there wasn't much thinking necessary). I was dying to know who was sick, though I thought I had an idea.

That probably sounds pretty horrible. After all, this was someone's life we were talking about. But the truth was that it felt like a game to me. *Correctly guess who has cancer and you win…a new car!* Only the prize was far less tangible.

On any given week day there were four waitresses scheduled to work. There were seven of us altogether. Nobody was perfect, but we had a really good bunch here.

Kayla walked past, burdened down by several newly-refilled glass ketchup bottles to put in the cooler. You'd be surprised by how heavy they can get when they are full.

Kayla was a slip of a thing, brunette, young – only a couple of years older than me. And like me, she took obvious pride in her appearance. When Kayla came into work, her apron was spotless, her uniform immaculate, her hair was up in a ponytail with her American flag headband around her forehead to keep the flyaways under control, and her makeup was done. The dishwashers had nicknamed her "Rosie the Riveter" because of that headband.

Kayla was quick to laugh and cut up with the rest of us, but was just as capable of staying focused on her customers and their meals. She was always smiling – a genuine smile, you know? That's part of what made her so great at what she did.

Most of the other waitresses, myself included, would slap a smile on our faces, make small talk, while mentally urging our customer to hurry up. It's not that we don't like our customers, it's just that when a person is doing 20 things at once; every extra second wasted throws off his or her timing, which is everything to a server. One can get mighty cranky even if he or she doesn't show it.

But that was what was different about Kayla. She really cared about each customer. She was that waitress who would welcome you in, prop her hip against your booth, and make you feel like you were coming into her home for lunch; as if she had all the time in the world. I don't know how she managed it, but I liked to watch her sometimes to see if I could pick up a few tricks.

Kayla was so vibrant and healthy, I instantly dismissed her from the list.

Over at the round table on the center tile sat Jazmin. She was hunched over as she recorded her tips and ticket sales for the day and filled out her time card.

Jazmin was a head-bobbing, finger snapping black woman, who was a force to be reckoned with. Her mood changed quickly, and you didn't always see it coming, but it never lasted long. She'd bite your head off one minute, and joke with you the next. As long as she was calling you "boo," you were okay.

She was always courteous and professional with the customers. Though she had a tendency to buck authority, she and Meghan got along relatively well…enough to keep the peace anyways.

I watched Jazmin arch her back, arms stretching over her head, and groan as she worked out the kinks. Was this simply the effect of working a long day on hard floors, heavy lifting, and nowhere to sit? Or, was this a sign of something more ominous?

I shook my head as I straightened my own back, as if stretching was as contagious as a yawn.

I grabbed up the silverware I had finished rolling as – I wanted to get out of there and deposited them in the bin. There wasn't much left for Kayla to roll, I retrieved my purse and phone, and, after checking with Meghan, walked out to my car.

The opening waitress, Esther, had been cut a few hours before. She was my front-runner in this morbid, mental game show. By far the oldest server here, she outdistanced the rest of us in age by anywhere from twenty to forty years, although she managed to wait circles around most of us.

She had arthritis in her hands and shoulders, which made opening bottles and carrying heavy trays difficult for her. The pain she was in by the end of the day could make her a little surly, which she tended to take out on the other waitresses. In deference to her age and experience (16 years at Daisy Mae's alone), we took it with a grain of salt.

Having worked so long at the same restaurant, Esther had a following of loyal customers, who would refuse to sit in anyone else's section; often going so far as to leave the restaurant entirely if Esther wasn't working.

Esther being sick made the most sense to me. She was older, wasn't in the best of health, and if it she was having side effects from the cancer, they could easily be explained away by other ailments. I didn't know much about cancer, but I decided to keep an eye on her for the next couple of days and see if anything popped out at me.

I was off the next day, but I stayed true to my word. When I got back to work, I spent the next two days watching everyone, especially Esther.

The first waitress I saw when I got back was a lady named Pam.

Pam was a sweetheart. She was a little bigger than most of the servers on staff, but, if anything, it complimented her big heart. She radiated warmth and caring and could always be called upon to lend a helping hand when one of us got overwhelmed.

Pam was the momma of the group. She had the best advice, the calmest nature, and the biggest smile. Her oldest son, EJ, bussed on the weekends when it got too busy for us to clear our own tables.

Out of every single person working in Daisy Mae's she was the only one whose marriage had stood the test of time. Pregnant at 17, she and her boyfriend, Joe, had raced to the altar. Sixteen years, two children, and 50 pounds later, she and Joe were still just as content and in love as they had been on the day of their marriage. You could tell that Pam was comfortable with her life, and those warm feelings radiated over onto the rest of us. Every day working with Pam was a little more pleasant than it would have been without her.

Today Pam was cutting up lemons in the service area when I walked through the door. We exchanged pleasantries as I washed my hands and fixed myself a drink before starting my shift.

I briefly considered Pam, but just as quickly crossed her off the list. She was a good candidate in theory, but one thing everyone knew about Pam was that she wore her heart on her sleeve. With that peaceful expression on her face, you just knew that there was nothing so bad in her life that she couldn't easily push it to the side while she was at work.

Tonya and Sarah were different stories.

Tonya was still an enigma to me; she felt closed off somehow. She was still pretty new. In fact, she had only been hired about a week after I was. There were a couple of noticeable differences when you compared her with the rest of the girls, however.

For starters, she was the only waitress who hadn't had any waitressing experience when she was hired. This made for an awkward transition. Waitressing can be tricky. You have a dozen steps or more that you need to follow per table. Those steps are constantly rearranging themselves depending on the customer, the speed of the kitchen, and how and when your other tables are seated.

A lot of restaurants will only give a waitress four or five tables, limiting the complications, but here at Daisy Mae's each waitress could have as many as eleven tables at any time. This can be hard on the most hardened of waitresses, let alone a new hire.

The other thing about Tonya, and by far more noticeable to us Southerners, was the fact that she wasn't one of us. She had moved down here from Maine to take care of her mother. More than once, I'd heard her joke about being called a Yankee; and it was probably true. Anyone was fair game to us if they didn't have the Southern drawl, call soda, Coke (regardless of brand), and root for either the Georgia Bulldogs or the Auburn Tigers. She had probably been called a Yankee every day since moving here.

Whether that was the reason she felt so closed off, I didn't know; but she was definitely hiding something. I had a feeling, though, that she was just protecting herself from people who hadn't fully accepted the "foreigner."

On the other hand, Sarah was a little too friendly. She was constantly coming in with hangovers. She was always joking about something. I'm not sure she even knew how to be serious. But her joking manner could get her in trouble, too. She never took into account who she was joking with or whether they would find it funny. She'd been written up more than once for just such errors in judgment.

Like with Tonya, I had a theory on Sarah's actions. Her behavior was too consistently one note and happy. It seemed fake. Every once in a while I thought I could see a chink in her armor. Whether it took a second too long for her to put her smile back on or her grin would get brittle after a particularly trying event, every once in a while I felt like I could see what was really going on in her head. It wasn't always pretty.

But maybe, I was just overanalyzing. Perhaps, she really was just a shallow, party girl.

I don't know which I would rather have believed.

Putting that thought from my mind, I watched Esther closely for the rest of the day. After studying all the girls, Esther was still in the top spot. She seemed the same as any other day, but I wasn't looking for changes in her, I was looking to find clues in her daily actions that I might have missed.

As I watched her, I noticed a million tiny things that could mean anything or nothing: the way she collapsed on her break, the way she gulped down water like she was dying of thirst or the way she popped pain pills like they were breath mints.

There was nothing for it, but to confront Esther. This was probably a tactless decision, but I had come this far. I needed to see it through. My curiosity would not be put off.

My chance came after closing. Esther, Pam, Kayla, and I were working that day. Pam opened. It had stayed so busy, though, that no one had gotten cut early. As we all went about our side work, Esther came up to me, "Let's grab a smoke right quick, honey."

This was a ritual of ours. If we weren't too focused on getting done and going home, the smokers would go out and grab a quick drag.

"Let me grab my smokes," I said.

We went out back and sat down. I was back in the chair by the air conditioner.

I was a little nervous now that the time had come. So, rather than saying anything eloquent, I just blurted out; "I know you're sick."

Esther looked at me, eyebrows slightly raised. "Excuse me, honey," she said. "But you don't know squat."

I opened my mouth, closed it again, not sure where to go from there. She hadn't denied it, technically. Should I try asking her straight out? That hadn't worked so well the first time.

Esther looked forward, almost distantly, her face serious. "I am an old woman."

I waited to see if she would say more. I was a gossip, but I would only push so far, and no farther. If she didn't want to talk, I couldn't and wouldn't force her.

"You're right," she said. "I'm sick." She took a drag of her cigarette. "I'm an old woman with a list of problems a mile long…but I've talked to Meghan and Leslie, and I know a mite more about what goes on in this restaurant than you. And, I know what you're not sayin'."

I trained my eyes on Esther's face. I had already made a fool of myself in her eyes. The best thing I could do right now was to be forthright.

She turned her head and looked me in the eyes. I knew what she was going to say before she said it. "I don't have cancer."

Esther didn't say anything else. She stood up, put out her cigarette and went inside.

I stayed outside for a minute, frustrated and confused. If it wasn't Esther, I didn't have a clue.

That's when the door opened back up. I thought maybe it was Esther coming back, but Kayla walked out the door.

She stood there hesitantly. I knew she was uncomfortable. Smoke from my cigarette curled up and floated toward her. "Esther just told me about what you said."

My brows furrowed as a niggling suspicion rose the hair on my arms and neck.

"It's me." Kayla looked me straight in the eye, just as I had done with Esther, and shock jolted my system.

Kayla?

For the first time, the magnitude of the disease really struck me. I had assumed that it would be someone older, someone in poorer health. I had thought there would at least have been a clue, but Kayla had never let on. She never slowed down, never took a sick day. She must have scheduled her treatments for off days and after work. It had never even crossed my mind that it could have been her. Did she even have health insurance?

"How?" I asked.

For crying out loud, she never stopped smiling! Surely cancer patients were supposed to frown every once in a while.

"I was diagnosed with uterine cancer ten months ago. They caught it early and took everything out, but the cancer spread to my fallopian tubes."

I couldn't help but continue to stare, with my mouth hung open. She was standing there, telling me so matter-of-factly that she had *cancer*.

The foundations of my world were rocking and she acted like it was no big deal!

"But you seem so normal," I whispered.

"I am normal. I just happen to have cancer."

I felt like a part of me had gotten sick with her. We could almost be the same person. We were almost the same age, the same hair color, and similar height.

"But shouldn't the cancer make you sick?" I asked, grasping at straws.

"I am sick," she said. "I'm sick, I'm tired, and my hair is falling out. That's why I wear the headband. I have to keep a toothbrush in my car in case I throw up in public. But it's not the cancer. You'd think it would be, but it's not." She paused. "I didn't feel sick when I found out I had this. The cancer made me sick, but the chemo and radiation made me *feel* sick."

She looked back at the door. I wasn't going to get much more out of her, and I wasn't sure I wanted to. I felt nauseous.

"In a way I'm glad this happened. I can't hide it for much longer. Not physically. I wasn't sure how to tell everyone, so thank you for giving me the out."

I gaped at her as she turned and went back inside; my eyes welled up with tears. She seemed so healthy. In fact, I was less healthy than she was. I smoked! I was smoking now! I took short cuts at work and slacked off and…If this could happen to someone so inherently good, it could happen to me.

I threw my cigarette on the ground and stomped it out, disgusted and horrified and panicked.

Kayla had cancer, but she just kept smiling.

Choices

By Jeanie Davis, MS survivor

So many nights I lay awake
Wondering what tomorrow will hold.
How will I keep commitments I've made?
Will I stand firm? Will I fold?

Will I have the power to battle the day?
Will I have the strength then to win?
Or will I be forced to sit this one out,
And yield to the battle within?

Stripped of my dignity, stripped of my pride,
Stripped of the person once me.
Still nothing can strip me of choices I make
That determine the person I'll be.

The choice to count blessings instead of regrets,
The choice to look forward—not back.
The choice to keep fighting and never give up
When I feel I am under attack.

Drive to Thrive

The choice to look pity square in the face
And never succumb to its call.
The choice to serve others; feel love and know joy—
To be happy in spite of it all.

My Constant Companion

By Shaunna Gonzales

"Have you considered you might have multiple sclerosis?"

"What?" My jaw manages to form the single syllable while my world collapses.

"I mention it because your eyes dart around like my mother's and she has MS," Dr. Samuels continues rubbing my neck before he twisted it. Snap, pop. It's a good thing Dr. Samuels is an excellent chiropractor.

"I can't possibly have MS." I argue because I've never fainted. I have all of my fine motor skills. I don't bump into things. My balance is a little off, but I don't have time to be sick. I'm just feeling the heat early this year. Right. It's March in southern Nevada and not in the triple digits yet.

"I'm not a specialist. I can give you a referral. I think you should check it out."

*****

Two weeks later I'm sitting in one of the neurologist's patient rooms, thankful the barrage of tests is behind me. It's been a long day, starting with MRIs across town, including the contrast yuck they inject. Though one must lie perfectly still, it is not relaxing due to the loud, constant "clunk, clunk, clunk" of the huge magnet half-orbiting my head to picture every slice of my brain. That had been the easy test; the ones that followed in the neurologist's back room must have been designed to create a massive failure for even the most tempered, over paid, desk jockey of all time. I figure they let me off the hook when I pretty much blew three tests in a row.

I hear the doctor outside the door, shuffling large sheets of x-ray type negatives. He walks in without them–not a good sign. Apparently he has determined that I don't deserve any explanation of what the films show.

"Well, Mea, the films are conclusive. You have multiple sclerosis." My world had already collapsed, now my mind goes blank. I sit there, stunned to a complete meltdown of thought.

"Can you tell me when you went blind?"

Huh-what? "Um, I've never gone blind." Is he kidding me?

"Actually, the largest scar is behind your right optical nerve. You did go blind, if only temporarily." He pauses, waiting for my response. I stare at him in disbelief. "I realize it may have only been for roughly 36 hours, but you did go blind. That kind of scarring would traumatize the optical nerve."

I spend the rest of the exam in shock, coming back to a semblance of coherency when he offers me his assistance to leave.

"You go home and rest. Think about what I've said and try to remember when you went blind. That may help us track how long you've had MS."

*****

Even worse than reporting the doctor's findings to my husband, Harrison, is coming to grips with reality. I have a sister who has lived with MS for roughly 30 years. The reunion when my older siblings decided to relieve her of motherhood responsibilities by doling out her children still haunts me. My sister, dealing so gracefully, is my role model. I praised her once, even going so far as to claim my willingness to have the same disease if I could be just like her. I'd been young and didn't realize what I was saying.

Now I shiver with terror. She fights her loss of balance, motor skills, cognitive powers, and refuses to succumb to needing a wheelchair except for the months she convalesced after falling and breaking her hip while hanging clothes on the clothesline. News of her heart attack scared the logical thought process from my brain for weeks. MS isn't hereditary, so how did I get it? What symptoms will haunt me?

The specialist assures me that I might not go blind permanently, but it is a possibility. Then the cretin *smiles* and delivers his next blow, "Do what you can now because when you one day occupy a wheelchair, you'll never get out." The louse didn't even have the bedside manner to use "if."

Thanks, Doc. My baby needs me. Cradling my one-year-old baby in my arms, I gaze at his innocent face. How much of his life will I miss? I missed his first step while a friend cared for him. I was busy being poked, prodded, filmed, and generally tortured by specialists just because I'd had a major heat stroke last summer. Only now I recognize it for something much more sinister; I'd almost died.

A tear glistens on my baby's cheek and I realize it isn't his. If I go blind, I'll never see his first day of school, his first baseball game or home run. I'll never see him become a man or the beauty he will marry. The tears are freely flowing as I think of not just this one, but all of my four children. I may miss it all. Of course I've been around the disease enough to know that the odds are not good when it comes to a wheelchair, and that contraption isn't the final one. Most MSers (multiple sclerosis patients) are in scooters or worse, bed-ridden.

At that moment, a contrary memory splits my core. I'd gone blind on my 19th birthday. I'd been working at the Grand Canyon. There had been no pain and yet I'd assumed that after staying up to watch the sunrise, I'd cut my cornea via my contact lens again. Unlike previous times when I'd slept overnight with my lens in and cut my cornea, this time I didn't experience any pain. At the time the nurse hadn't seen any reason for the blindness, but she had patched my eye anyway.

Swallowing my tears, I reach for the phone and dial the doctor's number.

*****

Bracing myself for the seasonal heat wave, I order the 30 saplings to shade our back yard from sweltering heat and start digging. The hard pan denies me for days and yet I refuse to give in. I know better than to stay in the heat as it will drain every ounce of energy from me, but I must do it now, before the next attack of my silent killer. While Harrison sleeps days to work nights, the children remain indoors in the refrigerated air and care for the baby since I'm no longer nursing. I toil, digging the trench for the water line. Digging gives me time to wonder why Harrison doesn't help and somehow I realize it's just easier for him to say nothing, denial—the ugly beast robs me of my confidant.

My older son brings me a 2-liter bottle of water. I drink about half of it, remove my wide-brimmed hat, and pour the rest over my head, relishing the refreshment that does nothing to lower my core temperature.

"It's hot out here," my son complains.

"It is, but at least I don't have to dig down another foot for the frost line." I spend the next few minutes explaining what a frost line is and that in southern Nevada it is merely inches compared to Idaho's 18 inches or more. He can relate to this as we have lived in Idaho and Utah with their cold, snowy winters.

"Mom, you look real tired. Are you sure you should be doing this?"

"Son, the doctor didn't say I couldn't. He said I better keep doing what I can while I can. Tomorrow I might not be able to do it."

He takes the shovel from my hands and I watch him dig five feet of trench in the time it takes me to do half as much. I thank him and try to retrieve the shovel. He doesn't let me. Stubborn eleven-year-old, his Irish-

German is showing. Not having any Irish, I'm not the match for him I'd been before this project.

One-hundred-and-fifty feet and 30 trees later, I'm too exhausted to finish the job. My strength has dissolved to fatigue.

*****

The task of planting trees and digging water lines mostly done, I return to the doctor. He fills out the form for my handicap placard and wheelchair. I send in the form for the placard, but refuse to live in a wheelchair.

According to studies endorsed by the National Multiple Sclerosis Society, there is no cure for MS and yet for months I joke with doctors about my plight.

Refusing to accept the inevitable, I secure a part-time job with Dr. Samuels, the chiropractor who recognized my darting eyes symptom. He hires me for the duration of the summer until his receptionist returns from her long vacation.

Thunder and lightning fill the desert atmosphere with electricity. A flash flood alert streams across the television moments before I dash out the door for work one morning.

"Boys, no four-wheeling today. I need you home to take care of your little sister and the baby." Although there are groans of disappointment, they agree and I'm off to dodge the worst of the huge raindrops to get to work.

Unable to run, I do my best to hurry from the parking lot, down the breezeway and into the office. I arrive, totally drenched.

"Did you leave any water in the rainclouds?" Dr. Samuels teases.

"Yeah. I had to hurry though. Did you bring me your lightning rod?"

"Sorry, didn't think you were serious."

"Hey, whatever will work. Of course I'd probably need the rod in one hand and a scorpion in the other while standing on the highest bluff. If

I survive, I should be cured of MS. Right?" My feisty rebuttal signals my energy level for the day. It is a quiet day. Most people will live with their back pain until the rain lets up. Desert rats.

*****

Rain drizzles all day, draining little color from the gray skies overhead. I smile at the contrast between western Washington and southern Nevada. A dozen years have marked their time since my diagnosis and although I spent a winter in my wheelchair, I refuse to stay there. Walks to the back door to let the dog out became walks to the corner, and eventually around the block. The dog, though adopted under the doctor's advice not to have one, has kept me mobile.

I stagger down halls, bumping and bruising arms, hips and legs but I hate the wheels that offer their support while threatening my freedom. Of course my pride comes into play. I hate having people doting over me like I'm dying. They are welcome to look. As long as I don't see their expressions, it doesn't bother me. But those who know me make sure they ask how I'm doing. I hate that, so my chair stays hidden now that we have moved to Washington.

As skies clear somewhat and temperatures warm for the spring and summer season, I am in my front flower garden, sitting on my jacket, digging in the dirt. No one knows me in this new neighborhood and I have Harrison at my side. A neighbor who we have met only once comes by and stops to chat. Somehow the conversation comes around to why I can't manage to get to my feet. *Dang MS.*

"I'd be more than happy to help you up."

"Thanks, but…." Since MS is so close to Ms. (the abbreviation for miss, or Mrs. and pronounced *miz*) I call it a "she." I know better than to open my mouth when I'm tired and yet "she" just can't wait to take center stage.

"Ms. MS is going to keep me here on the ground until Harrison takes me inside."

"You have MS?" The new friend is totally shocked. "For how long?"

Now the quick answer is never enough for Ms. MS. She must commence a well-practiced, but poorly executed dissertation of how, why and when she arrived on the scene…my scene. Somewhere near the end of the lengthy explanation, I gain a semblance of control over the wagging jaw I share with my interloper.

"I refuse to give up and die, or in my case retire to die in a wheelchair. That just isn't my style."

"Oh wow, you are my new hero," the neighbor sounds like I've obtained superhuman status.

I instantly feel embarrassed. Why can't I manage to be quiet about my disease? I know the answer; I probably included it in my overly long oratory.

"According to the NMSS (National Multiple Sclerosis Society), MS hits active young adults in their late twenties to mid-thirties. MS affects balance, motor and cognitive skills, energy, and pretty much every body function. 'Active' describes me prior to the onset of MS quite well with the dancing, horseback riding, interior decorating, crafting and singing that filled my free time. The time stamp is more than a bit off in my case, but although that first scar showed up at 19, I wasn't diagnosed until 40…."

At this point I have a moment to chastise myself and warn the unsuspecting neighbor. Of course Ms. MS keeps me from successfully verbalizing the alert due to the speech and cognitive challenges I deal with. "Back away from the jabbering idiot. She can't catch you. Go now."

Ms. MS takes over again and I hear myself tripping over most of my words as my brain and mouth refuse to work in harmony. Dang cognitive glitch. Harrison at last comes to the rescue, jumping into the conversation and effectively shutting me down.

Whew, my blabbering was getting embarrassing.

Night comes and with it my usual tirade of uncontrollable emotions as I try to verbalize them, unsuccessfully. Only when I'm lying down do I calm down to express my true feelings or what I can make of them.

"I don't know sweetheart." I'm trying to backpedal and apologize for my outburst moments earlier. "I just can't stop myself. I yell and scream at the kids. No wonder our oldest son refused to move when the rest of the family moved north, opting to stay with friends to finish high school. The next oldest son dropped out of school and followed a job opportunity in California before he graduated as well. I can't blame them."

"Then why don't you stop?"

"I try to, really I do." The inability to control ones emotions is just one of the many symptoms of the disease. One may be aware of it and still not manage to govern it.

"There just has to be a cure or if there isn't, at least something that will help. You know the drugs have never helped. I watch my diet. You know how many things I've given up."

I don't wait for him to respond to the variety of sub-topics; at this point I'm on a roll again. He knows it is safer to just let me go. My mind illogically tackles the issue of depression which I believe I've mastered.

"If there were just something that would help like the full spectrum light helped the depression, things would be so much better."

"Sweetheart, you're tired." He's doing his best in the eye of the storm. I'm winding up again.

"Just shoot me or fix me. Is that too much to ask?"

"I'd never shoot you. Thump you sometimes, but never shoot." He pulls me close and gently thumps the top of my head. Usually this is comforting, but tonight the ugly irrational monster is in and I burst into uncontrollable sobs. I pull away noticing how much it hurts to even let him touch me, which only inflames my vituperative self, inflaming everything I know or think I know. At last I dissolve into blubbering tears, ashamed of myself and of losing control.

"Get some rest. Tomorrow you have an appointment with your new neurologist."

I cringe, forcing down my unexplainable fear of driving to the doctor's office less than three miles away. I sniffle and roll over, trying to find a comfortable way to sleep. It's a restless night with my full body pain and feet twitching at irregular intervals.

Why has this happened to me? I delve into the familiar question as I do on many sleepless nights unwilling to take comfort in any answer my mind manages to land upon.

*****

This neurologist is slightly different from the last, he is exhausting all other possibilities before confirming the diagnosis I received 12 years prior.

I pull into a parking space, my hands trembling. The drive has been uneventful and yet I'm a wreck. I retrieve my cane, angry to have to own one. At least I didn't have to park in the disability parking today. I try not to as often as I can.

My mood is improved to a quiet acceptance of my plight for the moment as I wait to be called from the waiting room. Dr. Williams doesn't make me wait long.

"The tests for Shogran's came back negative so it is a good thing that we sent you in for the MRIs." My fists clench involuntarily remembering how I'd used my last muscle relaxers to be able to cope with the clunking magnet. Thank goodness I hadn't had the dreaded copper taste to deal with while trying to relax for the half hour to 45 minute, touch-less torture.

"So, do you believe me now that I have MS?"

Momentary uncertainty whisked across Dr. Williams' expression, confounding his bedside manner for a moment before he pasted his pleasant expression back in place.

"We've been looking for everything 'but' for a while now, haven't we? In that time, I feel we've become friends, don't you agree?"

"Uh, huh." I didn't agree, but I wasn't about to burst his bubble.

"Mea, multiple sclerosis isn't a killer, but you know that. There's a reason I've tested you for everything under the sun before coming to this diagnosis. Quite frankly, it's a slam to my ego and pretty much any doctor's ego to basically tell a patient they have MS. It's like saying, 'I'm sorry, there is nothing I can do for you, except prescribe overly expensive drugs. You are now slated for a very long and painful death.' Long as in, 'until death do us part,' and painful because the nerves are taking a hit and dying every day. Think of a spindly plant that is reaching with all its might for the beauty of the sunlight and its life giving rays only to be singed a little every day. The plant doesn't die instantly, it lives out its full life cycle the best it can until frost or something else kills it." I knew from his tone that it was a prepared speech; it didn't match his fraudulent smile.

"There are experimental drugs coming on the market, but quite frankly, your number is up. The fact that your first exacerbation was over 25 years ago and you are still mobile is very unusual, not to mention your energy levels and relatively low pain. The next flair you have may be the one that ends your run. I don't know if it will be today, tomorrow or next week, but the odds are that it will come. I recommend you do the blood tests now so that when the new drug becomes available you will be at the front of the line, so to speak."

Fatigue keeps me from punching him in the stomach. Gee, thanks Doc, for being so positive. I go home to work in my garden, basically pulling weeds until I'm too tired to drag myself indoors. The children had tried to help me inside without success, so the yard is where Harrison finds me in yet another round of tears when he gets home.

As he carries me up the steps to our bedroom, I find the cognitive function to thank him for his assistance in the yard, the kitchen and now to bed. I refuse to let him help me in the bathroom, hoping to save a smidgen of romantic dignity. He tucks me into bed.

"Sweetheart." Hubby dares to have a logical conversation with an illogical MS-er. "You've heard me mention Oliver at work."

Nice one. I don't know Oliver though he's been mentioned often so I can't verbally attack the man. "Yeah."

"He's got an aunt who has gone through this protocol a while back and he says she's doing really well. He says he would be willing to share some reading material if you're interested. Remember how he mentioned a Dr. Huggins or Higgins or something like that?"

I nod noncommittally. I've heard about every outlandish, farfetched cure for MS that has ever been thought of, including bee stings, absurd diets, lightning, and scorpion stings just to name a few. Most things have no science behind them.

Harrison showers this latest cure with cautious accolades. This is something he never does. Two days later he hands me a thin booklet.

"This is where we start. I read most of it over my lunch hour and it makes sense. You should read it."

I cautiously acquiesce and agree with Harrison's conclusion. The next step is to become better informed. I purchase the doctor's book and read it, including all the reference material he uses, at least what I can get my hands on and almost as quickly forget most of the information except the distinct feeling that the protocol to have the metal, especially the mercury amalgams and root canals, removed from my mouth will benefit me personally. The next step is finding a qualified specialist and scrapping our pennies together. It will require over $4,000.00 as the insurance companies consider the protocol experimental or "cosmetic." As if being able to walk and stand without losing one's balance is purely cosmetic.

*****

Two years later, I wondered if the day for the procedure would ever come. I've handled every "nay-sayer" as diplomatically as one struggling to retain cognitive functions possibly can, including not referring to "Huggins Applied Healing" by name. I know the protocol sounds like it couldn't possibly work, but I've read the research, albeit I promptly forgot most of the technical jargon. My memory often reminds me of the first admonition to consider heavy metal poisoning long before my diagnosis. They didn't have the facts and I cast it aside with all the other wild cures. Third time's the charm, or so the saying goes, that was when I listened, read and became informed.

I found a specialist and drove five hours one way often enough to know the traffic patterns. The amalgams were removed, the highest negatively charged at a time. I then took time to heal before the major surgery was done, without pain killers—the removal of root canals. Special protocol was followed for those specialized dental visits.

Why is it that powerful forces don't want those living with auto-immune diseases to know the truth? The protocol, as farfetched as it may sound to some, has worked for me.

I've changed my eating habits including denying myself of favorite foods including but not limited to anything with gluten in it, oatmeal, fish, pork and the killer, I say that sarcastically, chocolate. Much of the dietary changes have come slowly over the years long before learning of Huggins and his protocol. After staying away from the specific food items for over a year, any little slip is painful enough to enforce total compliance. Eating right has only been my part of the recovery process in addition to refraining from the use of anything that contains aluminum, as in replacing pots and pans, avoiding antiperspirants—which means deodorants and daily showers, changing toothpaste brands and anything else I can bring myself to avoid. I will continue following the regime for as long as I choose to feel good.

I'm proud to say that I have followed every specification of doctor's guidance, including one year of doing so little, I thought I might go stir-crazy. The guidelines were necessary in my case due to the heart meridian which the root canals sat on. That and, my father, and his mother, both died of heart attacks at young ages.

*****

I smile at Harrison across the dimly lit room. Yes, I've waited a long time for this moment to arrive. The bride's father taps the microphone to get the crowd to quiet.

"A word from the groom."

Our son steps forward in his tux, and clears his throat. "Most of you have met my parents tonight and well, in spite of Dad giving us a toast with sparkling cider, and my mom not drinking to his toast, I want to assure you that they really are great parents."

A gentle wave of laughter ripples over the group.

"And to prove just how normally abnormal they are, may I present my mom and dad."

A blue spotlight finds Harrison at the same time a slightly red one settles on me. The band strikes up a tango. I smile, knowing *I can do this.*

"Dad, don't drop her," our son teases as we approach the center of the dance floor. We've practiced for two months, nothing but tangos at the dance studio. At this moment, this dance expresses my victory with raw emotion embracing the best of life and the promises it yet holds.

Harrison and I dance as our children watch.

I smile while dancing remembering how I feared missing so many things. I didn't miss it. I held my baby's hand as he entered the school on his first day, just as I had with his siblings. I didn't go blind as I had feared, instead I witnessed his home run and laughed as other parents offered to pay him five dollars for another in the play-offs. I've attended the weddings of our older sons and see their beautiful brides.

I am confident that I will see their baby's first steps and laugh with them. I will hold grandbabies in my arms and play with them, not just listen to them play. Tears of thanks for Hal Huggin's will to fight his odds and think outside the MS Box often replace those of despair in the past, freely flowing as I enjoy all of my four children. I didn't miss it all.

MS is losing this battle. I refuse to give up and die.

From Mom to Me

By Ellen Gibbons

I am not too hard to find.
You will find me in the fragrance of sage after the rain.
You will find me in the eyes of a newborn child.
You will find me in the stillness of a hawk
quietly readying herself for flight toward the mountain.
If you believe these things too hard to find,
look into your sweet soul.
I am there warming and hugging you gently,
my love for you silently
caressing your spirit.

Maggie

By Louise Laughlin

Maggie's parents, Amanda and Tyler, joyfully anticipated the arrival of their first child. She arrived May 29, 2012 in seemingly perfect health. When held and talked to, Maggie cooed and babbled in response. She had a calm, sweet personality like her parents.

One week before her mother's maternity leave ended, Maggie had a massive seizure. She stopped breathing and began to turn blue. After what seemed like an eternity, but only a minute in reality, she began to breathe on her own. Tears streamed down her mother's face as Amanda and Tyler rushed Maggie to the hospital. Maggie was immediately admitted to ICU. Her mother and father watched and waited as the staff put a video EEG (electroencephalogram) on her. The tests revealed that Maggie had experienced an interruption in her brain activity, but it was inconclusive as to the cause.

After her seizure, Maggie smiled and cooed as usual. Doctors conducted numerous tests including an MRI and a lumbar puncture. The initial diagnosis was infantile epilepsy, which the doctor said she could out grow by age two.

After three days, her parents were allowed to take Maggie home. They were urged to schedule follow-up doctor appointments and to keep a close watch for a reoccurrence.

Maggie's wise pediatrician, after reading the hospital reports, suspected infantile epilepsy and recommended Maggie be taken to a child epilepsy specialist. At the first appointment with the specialist, Amanda was dismayed at the doctor's observation of Maggie. "She's beautiful and looks healthy. The symptoms seem to indicate infantile epilepsy, but unless I can witness it happening and get more tests performed, there is little I can do at the moment."

Feeling dejected, Maggie's mother left his office. Just as Amanda pushed the button on the elevator outside the office, Maggie had a seizure and quit breathing. Amanda ran into the office yelling. "She's not breathing! Come, see. Now!" The doctor gave Maggie oxygen, and then rushed her to the adjacent hospital. He immediately ordered an EEG on the tiny eight-week old baby.

Hours later, the doctor said, "It appears likely that the diagnosis we've discussed is accurate. I'm changing her medications to try to prevent the seizures. We still need to conduct more tests to find the cause. Meanwhile, we need to monitor her closely."

Mounting hospital bills and Maggie's mother needing to quit her job to care for her caused incredible financial stress. Further, there was no pattern to Maggie's seizures, which caused her parents to alternate the task of watching her all through the night and day. Neither parent ever slept soundly causing them sleep deprivation and wondering when the next seizure would occur.

As Maggie grew, her seizures increased. So did her medications and trips to the hospital. There were occasions when Maggie had as many as 18 seizures in one afternoon. Each seizure caused her to stop breathing. The nurses and doctors who cared for Maggie treasured her. She thrived between episodes, always smiling, cooing, or babbling her little sing-song talk, but her normal child development was severely cut short.

Finally, Maggie's bedroom was set up with monitoring equipment and emergency oxygen. This safety net allowed her parents some normalcy in their daily life routines. She was required to wear a custom helmet to help shape her head that flattened on one side from her many days lying still in a hospital bed restrained by all of the monitoring devices. At first, she whimpered showing her displeasure when her flowered headpiece was put on her, but quickly accepted it without protest.

When friends tell Maggie's parents how impressed they are with the affectionate way they handle their worry and constant care, they simply answer; "It's all we know and we love her." In fact, they adore her.

Days before her first birthday, a final diagnosis was confirmed. Maggie has a missing chromosome which causes her seizures and other challenges such as impaired sight. While this discovery did little to explain what Maggie's prognosis would be, it did qualify her to move up on the waiting list to see an epileptologist, who handled only special cases.

The epileptologist changed Maggie's medication again and placed her on a special diet; both of which have helped Maggie's growth process.

At 14 months, Maggie learned to roll over and hold her head up. Sometimes her arm would get stuck under her body when she rolled over. It took courage from everyone who watched to not help her. Maggie worked at it until she succeeded in getting her arm out from under her body. This precious baby continues to have physical therapy three times per week where she is learning to crawl. The two times per week occupational therapy is helping her to learn to play with toys and perform all the milestone tricks we often take for granted.

To date, she has endured three lumbar punctures, numerous hospital stays, and untold seizures. Yet her happy nature, and her drive to thrive continues. She overcomes obstacles with courage and determination. With God's help and the continued love and support from her family, all who know Maggie believe she will catch up and make a full recovery.

My Footprints

By Estee Woods

My cancer journey started four years before my birth when my grandma was diagnosed with breast cancer and given six months to live. Her name was Virginia, and she battled the disease for four years. She didn't just fight to live; she fought to live the life she loved. She didn't let cancer stand in her way. She got up every morning and made her husband breakfast. In fact, the day she died, she got up and went to the kitchen. A massive stroke spread paralysis throughout her body, and she exclaimed, "I will not live as a half a person." She died that afternoon. She was 50 years old.

My mom's breast cancer diagnosis came when I was three, so I spent my whole life knowing the word "cancer" too well. Her name was Barbara, and she also fought for four years. Her struggle centered on her three young children. She fought to make memories, to teach life lessons, to leave an imprint of love that would be strong enough to last our lifetimes. When the end came, it came quickly. She didn't fade slowly away. She was Mom until the morning she died; her whole life compressed into 33 years.

At 28, I was the proud mother of three kids; the oldest a five-year-old boy. That's when I found the lump. At 14 weeks pregnant, I got the results of my biopsy: breast cancer. The next five heart-wrenching months I went through eight rounds of chemo, knowing each time that my treatment poisoned my unborn baby. The night following each treatment I pushed at my stomach, over and over, trying to get my baby to move so I would know that she was still alive. Sometimes for an hour I'd beg her for a sign. And then I could feel her gentle swish, like she was saying, *Leave me alone, Mom, I'm trying to sleep.* Her name is Clare. She's beautiful. She's healthy. She just turned nine years old.

I gave a year of my life to cancer; it took over and the fear never left. There was another young mother I knew from church with a baby a few days older than my Clare. I would look at her jealously and think, *I bet she doesn't think about dying every time she holds her daughter.* But time passed. One year. Two. Five. I started to think maybe I'd won. Maybe I could raise my children and do what Mom and Grandma didn't—grow old. My husband and I had two more children. I had a great life. I was naive.

We went on a vacation to Newport Beach. I had one of those perfect moments; all six kids having fun together. I sat on the beach marveling at how beautiful life could be. Amidst this happiness, my fingers brushed against another lump; high, almost to my clavicle. I knew it was bad. The rest of vacation passed with a bitter-sweet edge. Life would change again when I got home. I had no idea.

The doctor appointment didn't scare me. Neither did the biopsy or even the new diagnosis. I'd been vigilant: a bilateral mastectomy, check-ups every six months. My last set of scans and tests had been five months earlier, right after the birth of my baby. Those results came back clean. This new tumor was small, and completely different from my first go round. The previous cancer hadn't come back. This was a new kind of cancer. At first glance the doctors staged it at one: easy-peasy. I wouldn't even have to do chemo. But I couldn't get two nagging thoughts out of my head: What if I don't get better this time? What if this is the tip of the iceberg?

Before my lumpectomy, the surgeon ordered a chest MRI. It showed a small, but suspicious mass in my lungs. A biopsy of that came back positive. Okay, two tumors. Maybe not as easy as I'd hoped. The oncologist was mystified that the cancer spread, but not in the usual manner: lymph nodes (the surgeon checked them during the lumpectomy and they were clean). So he ordered a PET scan. It was June 21. The first day of my favorite season. The day I found out I was dying. The cancer had metastasized all over my body.

I hate the phrase, "live like you're dying," because obviously whoever coined it has never been dying. It takes courage to start something, knowing I probably won't have a chance to finish it. It's depressing to look into a future that I know I won't be part of. I want to teach my baby to read. I want to see my son graduate from high school. I want to be there on my daughter's wedding day. I want to think about all the wonderful days that are just around the corner for my six kids. I want to live my life on my terms. I want to live like I'm going to be around for a long time.

So I fight, like my grandma and my mom did, before me. I struggle to be the mom I want to be. I take naps with my babies. I wear hats to piano recitals. I limp to swim meets. Cancer doesn't get any freebies from me. Lots of friends want to help—want to make meals or babysit my kids. No. If I can do it, I'm going to. I want to give every ounce of strength in my body to this life of mine. Cancer does not define me. My death is not the pinnacle of my story. Until I die, I'm alive!

No One Sea Turtle

By Garron Staten

My name is Leatherback. I'm a marine. First in. Last out. That's me. To be able to tell you this story is an accomplishment in its own right. There are those just like me, lost and forgotten. I wasn't supposed to make it out alive. No one sea turtle is destined to survive. I've been fighting since I was a hatchling. The Gulf (of Mexico) was my warzone. I was on the front line. We set up a perimeter to protect those on the inside. I wasn't assigned this task, but I knew that the job belonged to me. When you are in total darkness, the thoughts in your mind keep you company. Those are memories I won't soon forget. I cry often over those that were lost and I encourage those that will try.

In total darkness, I didn't know where I was or what I would become. Surrounded by thousands just like me, I was waiting on something.

That was my first thought. You see, if the sands are just the right temperature, a hatchling will develop as a male or a female. Anything below 82 degrees Fahrenheit, it will be male. Anything above 85 degrees Fahrenheit, it will be female. The only thing certain is that it will be.

After many days, so many that I couldn't keep count—maybe it was 40, or 60—

I knew it was time to escape.

Escape is another thought of the baby sea turtle. It uses its caruncle tooth to collapse its egg. It will absorb the yolk from its attached umbilical cord. This will provide enough energy for the impossible journey to the ocean.

I saw the darkness lighten as the ground around me opened up. I knew it was time, so I started to dig in tempo with my comrades. I did not want to be the first out of the hole, but I also did not want to be the last. Word from the front line said it was too hot and too bright to continue. Wait we must.

The temperature of the sand near the surface tells the baby sea turtles that it is too hot to surface. This means nighttime has yet to fall. They will wait a little longer, for two purposes: the sun will overheat them on their long journey and predators can't see them as well at night.

As darkness fell, we pushed forward, following the downward slope of the beach. I remember seeing a light glaring overhead. The rest is a bit blurry.

"Not that way!" I heard in the distance.

"No, that beast is getting closer!" I heard as something roared from behind me.

"Those winged creatures are diving fast!" was a warning that sent me running faster toward the horizon.

"Ghosts!" was a frantic call that scared even the bravest of us.

You see, we had to make a frantic run toward the water, using the natural slope of the beach, the white crests of the waves, and the light of the horizon as a marker. Coastal developments, such as hotels, are a false light indicator and can lead us astray. Those that follow the right direction will face other dangers. Raccoons chase us, sea birds fly overhead awaiting the moment that they can dive down and grab us, and the dreaded ghost crab will hide in the sand and ambush us, scooping us up with its one oversized claw.

No one sea turtle is destined to survive. Leatherbacks are the largest of all sea turtles. We are in a class of our own. Maybe that's why I survived. I'm no more valuable or important than any of my comrades. I did not possess talent or luck that kept me alive. Maybe it was because I had the drive. I do not need praise or parades or rewards. Instead, let those unnamed fighters be recognized now.

A note from the author about sea turtles:

Scientifically, the leatherback sea turtle is the largest sea turtle, growing over 1300 lbs. They are also one of the largest marine reptiles in the world. The leatherback literally is in a class of its own. Because it does not have a hard shell like other sea turtles, it falls under a different scientific classification. Temperatures of sand affect the sex of the turtles. Nests are usually warmer in the middle than along the outer rims, so those eggs closer to the edges are usually male. Sea turtles live all over the world with the exception of the Arctic. The males never return to their nesting place. Sea turtles really do cry! As salt can be harmful, they have developed special glands that excrete salt from the ocean water that they drink.

Fighting Four

By John Schwabenland

Louise, tired of squabbling all the time, hoped her chemo session might go smoothly for once. So far things were looking good. The blood tests were in, her records weren't misplaced, and the oncologist had signed all the papers.

The receptionist just informed her everything was set, and she along with one of her daughters stood grinning, half-stunned. Mary, the third oldest of her four girls, had flown in to Houston from Dallas and stayed the night with her in the old house, only to have to rise early and drive Louise down to the Texas Medical Center. Louise still drove herself around the neighborhood, but her 80-year-old eyes played tricks on her whenever she merged into fast traffic.

Mary guided her to a chair in the waiting area, helped settle her in, and said goodbye, reminding her as she left that Alice was on the way. Alice was the oldest, and Louise liked telling new acquaintances that if you take the first initial of each girl's name and placed them in correct order, the word ARMS was spelled.

Louise sat alone and read the novel she'd brought along. It was a suspenseful book so far, about the Salem witch trials. Alice arrived minutes later, drinking a Starbucks, palming an iPhone, and shouldering a big purse. Louise closed her book as her daughter leaned to give her a hug. Alice sat one seat away and used the empty chair between them as a table.

"Maybe I'll get out early today," said Louise. By early, she meant within five or six hours. There'd been days when the whole process took from eight in the morning until eight in the evening.

"We can sit here all day. I don't mind."

Louise nodded and thought this was all Alice would say for now, since her daughter appeared so busy with the phone. But then:

"As long as you don't go flying off the handle and curse someone when something goes wrong."

Louise glared at her daughter, who did not look up but continued scrolling and tapping. Alice had always been her right hand, ever since Louise's husband died 45 years ago, leaving her with seven kids. The youngest was six months then and Alice, in her thirteenth year, became a second mother to all the little ones.

"I don't curse people," Louise said.

"Mother…."

"What?"

"Nothing. Never mind." Alice said the "never mind" part in a falsetto voice, which Louise found infuriating.

A nurse soon appeared and took Louise back to one of the cubicles. There wasn't much room, but Alice, following closely, pulled up a hard plastic chair.

"Really, Alice, you don't have to stay," said Louise. The nurse hooked her up quickly and painlessly, and Louise was only bothered that her daughter had taken a day off from work and would be bored senseless. Her daughters made frequent sacrifices like this and then acted like it was nothing. Yet they all had hectic lives – careers and their own kids to look after. Louise always felt guilty for taking their time.

"I'm fine, Mom. Relax. Did I show you these pictures of Bryce?" Alice held her iPhone so that Louise could see the college graduation photos. Bryce was one of 14 grandchildren. All her kids and grandkids were smart and hardworking and so what had she done right? If she were one of the characters in the book she was reading, they'd indict her for invoking charms.

*****

Rebecca, the second oldest daughter, came to visit around noon. She was accompanied by Mary's daughter, Lizzy; they had been out shopping.

"Everything's going well I heard," said Rebecca. Louise knew the girls always texted each other, but how they could read those tiny messages was beyond her.

"She hasn't yelled at anyone yet, has she?" Rebecca said this jokingly to Alice, who shook her head and seemed to warn with her eyes.

Louise shook her head too. "Ha, ha. Don't listen to them, Lizzy. They're just out to get me. They persecute me."

"Sarah wants us to go out to eat tonight," Rebecca said, switching quickly. Sarah, the youngest of the four daughters, was still at work. "You up to it, Mom?"

"Sure, why not." The really bad effects of the chemo didn't kick in until two or three days later. She wouldn't mention how food didn't have much taste.

A few hours later Louise was home. She and the three oldest daughters sat at the kitchen table, while the granddaughter Lizzy lounged on the sofa in the den texting friends in Dallas.

The table they sat around was oak and oval, made to accommodate six. Not nearly as large as the old rectangular pine table they had in the past, with its long benches that sat three on each side. Giles, the oldest son, used to sit in the end seat opposite Louise's. They were like Pilgrims, or like the family in her book. But she sold that chipped and dinged old thing with its wobbly benches and rickety end-chairs thirty years ago in a garage sale. More recently, on the smaller table, she and the girls played cards. Contract rummy with quarter bets.

Cards!—a different battle altogether. Louise still played bridge at least once a week and even the younger, middle-age folk at the community center admitted she's a whiz.

Louise thought she could pretty much beat anyone.

Over a decade ago she taught her girls rummy, a much simpler game than bridge. When the daughters first started playing, they were mild and hesitant and Louise trounced them. Meekly they accepted their mother's complete mastery, her dominating play. She realized they were still learning the game but still she wondered: "Where's the fight in them?"

At last the daughters grew to understand the strategies and began themselves playing like Vegas high-stakes veterans, becoming tougher opponents. Yet Louise continued to win. Then her girls fought among themselves, criticizing each other's decisions. They scuffled every time they shuffled. Tiring of that, they teamed up and went after the champion herself.

"Whichever card you need, you get!"

"It's pure luck, the way you pluck."

"It's not luck, it's magic."

"Are you a good witch, or a bad witch?"

They thought this was funny. But eventually things flew out of control—on several occasions cards and profanities were hurled across the table. They stopped playing five years ago, two years after the diagnosis of her ovarian cancer. The emotions had become too volatile.

But hiding the cards—she'd tossed the rubber-banded decks onto the top shelf of the hallway closet—didn't stop the quarreling. Last Thanksgiving they set up extra tables in the den and the entire extended family came, toting cheesy vegetable casseroles, a honeyed ham, flour-dusted rolls…. Louise didn't have to stand on her feet cooking all day and the feast was wonderful—her daughters could conjure up dishes as tasty as her own. The dispute didn't arise until after the girls shooed everyone out of the kitchen and began cleaning. The four of them working together hardly allowed Louise to lift a finger, and it was then Louise said the dishwasher shouldn't be loaded that way.

"Don't just toss them in. Place the plates in the back, all in a row," she suggested. And it really was just a suggestion. "Then you'll have room for the bowls up front."

The other girls took offense and sided with Alice. They all said "Mother…" with lingering, pretentious exasperation. Then they told her it was impossible to get all the dishes in at one time and still have them come out clean. The tone of their voices seemed to imply that Louise was silly, that she didn't know what words came out of her mouth, that she was half-senile. Voices erupted and it turned out to be one of the nastiest fights she could remember. She rose, grabbed her walker, and left the kitchen. Wobbling through the den where the boys were watching football, she ignored the pleas behind her, her daughters' sudden vocalized contrition. One of the girls—it was Mary, the tallest one—scurried up and put her arm on Louise's shoulder.

"It's too late to be nice," Louise said, and she flicked her wrist and accidentally batted her daughter on the chin. Continuing to her bedroom, Louise locked the door, and refused to be consoled for the rest of the afternoon.

*****

Sarah, the youngest daughter, entered the kitchen, worn from work. She taught kids with special needs and had a tea-colored stain on the side of her white blouse.

"Hey girls. Hey Mom. I'm glad you didn't have any problems today."

"It's been nearly perfect," admitted Louise. "Except, my arm is starting to bruise."

"You're tough, Mom," said Rebecca, patting Louise on the back, rubbing in circles. "As many times as you've been beat up…." All her daughters were so affectionate. Louise thought herself the luckiest mother in the world.

"So where are we going to eat? I'm starved. Skipped lunch to get my lesson plans done."

"We're thinking about this Italian place."

"Sicilian."

"Same thing."

"No it's not."

And on the girls went, as Louise drifted off. She thought about all the things she had to get done tomorrow while she still felt okay. Balance her checkbook, go to Wal-Mart to pick up two birthday cards and three prescriptions and an HP-92 black ink cartridge for her printer, call about the $65 service/repair charge on her cable TV bill which she shouldn't have been charged for at all….

"She's spaced out."

"Mom?"

"Yes, I'm ready. Let's go."

"Let me help you up."

"No. I don't need help." Coordinating muscle movement in her hands, arms, legs, and what was left of her midsection after three operations, she rose. She grabbed her cane and followed the girls to Sarah's SUV, since it was last in the driveway.

*****

Alice collected money from the three younger sisters, laid the smaller dollar denominations on top the larger ones, and then exchanged them in her purse for a piece of gold plastic.

Louise snatched the bill.

"We've already taken care of that, Mom."

"But it's not the right amount." Louise was grateful they contributed for her order and wasn't going to fight about that, but still....

"We all looked over it," said Mary. "They double-billed Lizzy's entrée, but it's corrected at the bottom. See where the little negative sign is before the number?"

"She can't see anything that small," laughed Rebecca.

Sarah reached over with a fork and pointed on the slip of paper. "That means a credit."

"I know what it means. You all think I'm stupid."

"We gave money for the tip, too. 20 percent."

"Yes, and he was a good waiter. But I'm telling you it doesn't add up."

She tallied the numbers in her head, subtracting the credit along the way. The pre-tax total still came out $9.73 too much. And the erroneous higher total meant the tip was overdone by $1.95—not that she begrudged the young man a couple of bucks. The tax would be wrong, too.

The waiter came. Alice grabbed Louise's wrist, extracted the bill, placed the credit card on top, and handed it over.

Tears welled suddenly in Louise's eyes and her throat felt as though she were about to drown. Yet she wanted to say something to the waiter before it was too late.

"Be right back," he said.

*****

The SUV was stopped in her driveway, but Louise couldn't find the latch to open the door. Hadn't she got out earlier, at the restaurant? All by herself? Or had someone helped her? She felt muddled now.

"Pull up on it."

"On what? Where is the damned thing?"

"Hold on; I'll open it from the outside."

They snickered. Sometimes Louise laughed at herself, along with them—like whenever her wig slipped out of place. Now wasn't one of those times.

Inside the house Louise sat down with her girls to watch the last half of *Dancing with the Stars*.

They peacefully enjoyed the show—until one of her daughters said she liked the new guy, an actor who didn't act anymore, more than the retired football player. The other girls agreed, but argued about some of the females. Louise claimed the football player was one of the best ever, powerful but almost as light on his feet as the professional dancers—that's why he kept winning. And the girl she liked the best was the Argentinean, not the blonde. Two of her daughters sided with her about the Argentinean, but they all teased her about the football player, saying his muscles made him too stiff and they never liked him in the first place.

Louise came to a boil almost instantly.

"You don't know anything, any of you! Not the first thing about strength or winning!"

And loudly they argued back, too many at once. She couldn't tell one voice from another. Someone said it was ridiculous for her to get upset—yet they were all upset, too. Two of her daughters had high-blood pressure but were going at her fiercely as the others—Louise feared a vessel was about burst.

"Stop!" she screeched.

And whether it was her hoarse warrior anger or the fact the commercial break ended, they suddenly hushed. Glumly they watched the show drag to a close. Three of the girls migrated back to the kitchen to gather their purses.

"After 45 chemos you think she would have mellowed," one of them whispered.

"It's just like when we watched *Miss America* and she threw her score pad at the TV."

That never happened, but Louise thought it best not to say anything. Her daughters sometimes acted like hysterical teenagers, accusing her of things she never did. That's just how things started in Salem.

*****

Louise was still agitated, though it was almost midnight and the last of her daughters left the house three hours ago. That was Sarah, who hugged her and pecked her on the cheek.

She lay in bed unable to sleep, the fingers of her left hand closed in the pages of her book—there wasn't much sensation in those fingers anyway. She had popped an Ambien and thought it should have kicked in by now. It seemed so ineffective she wondered if she had mistakenly swallowed one of her other pills.

The historical novel she'd been reading for the last few days—but which she couldn't focus on now—centered on an Andover family whose mother was executed for practicing witchcraft. The heroine fought like hell to maintain her innocence, though a false admission would have made her life easier. That was in 1692, but Louise wondered why someone couldn't just go ahead and hang *her* right now? That's how miserable she felt and it had nothing to do with the chemicals she'd received. Only, the noose around her neck would slip entirely loose or the scaffolding beam would snap and splinter like a Popsicle stick. If seven years of stage-four ovarian cancer and four stubborn-as-hell daughters couldn't kill her, nothing could.

Those girls! Too full of opinions and emotions—she never knew what to think of any of them. All four were tough and successful and pretty as can be, and she loved them to no end. Though why couldn't they be more like her three boys, who helped, too, but were simple and silent and stayed out of her way, especially when she was irritated?

What she couldn't get out of her mind and irked her the most was the way the girls wound up ganging up on her, bickering at their old weakened mother who was now down to 113 pounds. The way they scolded her… it seemed they practically slapped her wrists. Was it just because she was now so tiny?

Tiny or not, she wasn't going to take it. She huffed and sat up straighter in her bed, pledging that tomorrow she wouldn't say a word to any of them. Not until they called and apologized first. And even then she'd be terse.

They want to fight? She'd show them how to fight. Then maybe after a week or so they'd remember she's their mother. The one who kept house while keeping all seven of them from killing each other. Who tweezed out a plastic peg jammed so far up one of their nostrils it couldn't be seen even with a flashlight, and who'd taken a knocked-out front tooth and rinsed it and jammed it right back in so that it re-took root and was as good as ever. All this while somehow budgeting the proceeds from an irregular income as a work-at-home watercolorist so that no one ever realized how poor they were. But transcending those enchanted deeds was this: She'd raised them so they weren't afraid to speak up and so they knew when to be feisty and when to downright scrap. Implicitly, by example, by simply being who she was, she taught them how not to be trampled or trumped. By anything. That's what they should recall.

After such consideration they would stop treating her like a child or a mental invalid or an evil hag—or whatever it was at the moment they regarded her as. But they would only stop for a while. Eventually they'd forget again—who she was and what she'd done for them.

Yet, even as they fussed, they'd be at her side. Every time. Every chemo session, every doctor appointment.

Here Louise paused in her thoughts, glancing down at the book in her hands. And following a blank moment—similar to one of her occasional mental lapses but much shorter—she laughed. It was like suddenly getting a punch line.

"My daughters," she said aloud. "My fierce little coven. They want to fight with me—against the cancer, the real enemy. But that's impossible. So their frustration comes out in squabbles, among themselves and with me." She shook her head, reprimanding herself.

"Why haven't I understood this before?"

She drew in a great volume of air, held it, and then exhaled slowly. The oxygen went straight to her brain, comforting her immediately.

"It's nice to finally make sense of things."

And now opening her witch book back to where she'd left off, she read herself to sleep.

A Quiet Sleep and a Sweet Dream

By Ellen Gibbons

A quiet sleep and a sweet dream.
If only we could be sure of this
when our time comes to leave this place.
Too often this hour is shrouded in a coat of tears
When each breath seems the last.
If only we could know.
If sad memories of the past could but be clouded,
The bright and shining moments would appear
As if joy were the only content
in what seemed a dark and stormy time.
If only we could remain youthful,
with unlined face and graceful hands;
Hands to hold others and only let go
when we are sure that those we love
are safe.

"Grandma, Go 'Round!"

By Pamela R. Goodfellow

Thirty some years ago, I hovered over my mother's hospital bed, and waited for her to open her eyes. When she did, the terror in them sent a knife through my heart, but I smiled quickly, assuring her that all was well. It wasn't, of course. A routine biopsy of a lump in her breast had resulted in an immediate double mastectomy. The doctors assured me that they had "gotten it all" but some further precautions would have to be made to complete the fight against the aggressive breast cancer that had invaded her body. I didn't tell her that then, as I smiled and wiped her tears and held tightly to her hand. Time enough for all that later.

Thank goodness times have changed. Over the last few decades magnificent progress has been made in the fight against breast cancer. My mother had the full deal, double mastectomy, incredible scars, long recovery, everything. Her doctors did not give her much hope, predicting that she had maybe a year to live. Always tenacious, Mom fought the good fight. She endured radiation, but could not handle chemotherapy. I remember a twinge of foreboding when we learned that the chemotherapy would have to be stopped due to the adverse effect it had on her liver. I pushed aside all thoughts that this did not bode well for the battle she faced. After months of watching her suffer, Mom achieved a measure of health. She was able to return to many of her regular activities and we, her family, released our collectively held breath and breathed a sigh of relief.

My children were small, not even school age, at the time of my mother's surgery. I have a picture of Mom, incredibly skinny and frail, holding my nine-month old baby girl. The contrast between my plump, healthy baby, and my painfully thin mother is almost too hard to bear. I keep it, even after all these years, to remind myself that although she is gone, she did successfully fight this horrible disease, and she did, for a while, thrive.

The first summer after her surgery, we attended Mom as best we could, ferrying her back and forth from treatments and our family summer home. She was weak and often in pain, exhausted by the treatments but determined to spend family time at our special place, on the shores of Lake Erie. We had traditions, some of which she could not yet do, and others that she was able to embrace. Our summer place was a big rambling old house on the Canadian side of the great lake. We, my three sisters and I, spent every summer of our growing up years, romping over the lawns, and spending hours building castles in the sand on the beautiful beach. Well, actually my little sister and I had a preference for sand-crafted horse ranches, complete with fancy barns, extensive paddocks and plastic horses galloping everywhere. And we all, including my mom, swam.

We swam in the rough waves, clinging to my father and watching my mother fearlessly face the breakers. We swam on the calm days, inventing water games, floating on inner tubes and reveling in the idyllic setting. In fact we swam in every kind of weather, and every condition that the great lake could throw at us. The lake house was the center of my family's life. It also held memories for us, both good and bad. My father, strong, loving and capable, died of a heart attack while cutting the back lawn the summer before my son was born. He never got to meet my darling children. My sister, once divorced and afraid of what life had to offer, married the love of her life on the graceful, sunlit lake-side lawn, with all of us in attendance. It was our retreat, our refuge and the place my mother felt most peaceful and serene. She drew strength from this rambling old house even when life threw challenges at her. Of course she would want to be there as she tried to heal from this massive surgery and fight her battle with cancer.

That first summer of her recovery, however, Mom could not swim. She could sit in a deck chair on the lawn, wrapped in blankets and a hat, looking out over the lake. The house is situated on high bank land, so the view from the lake-side lawn is magnificent. Two full flights of stairs lead to the sand and she could not manage them, until the very end of the summer. Late in August, with all our help, she made it down to the beach, and stood triumphantly for a few minutes on the sand. I have a picture of her, swathed in cotton shawls, surrounded by her daughters and grinning at the sunset. That one is not hard to look at.

The second summer after her mastectomy was different. She was better. She was doing physical therapy religiously, but still had trouble raising her arms above her head. Yet, she had gained weight, she looked frail, but healthy, and she wanted all of us to be with her at the summer house. My son was almost three and my daughter was not even two. They got to know their incredible grandma that summer. She spent hours sitting and talking with them, sometimes on the beach, as they built sand castles, sometimes on the back steps as they watched me grill hamburgers, and most every evening in the big Cape Cod chairs, on the lake-side lawn, as they watched the sunset. I don't know what these conversations were about, but over the years since she died, my children have revealed little things that they absorbed. Mom's influence was brief in actual time in their lives, but everlasting in their consciousness and in the man and woman they have become.

Maybe we all told them stories about that time, I am not sure. My favorite memory is my tiny, golden-haired daughter encouraging my mom to "run" around the house with her. The house was set on a gentle rise. The road-side had an entrance to the basement and a large flat acre of lawn. On either side of the house were sloping rises that led to the lake-side lawn. To encourage my mom to exercise, little Carrie would run up to her and say, "Grandma, go round?" My mom would flash her smile and rise up. Together, they would "run" to the right-side of the house and start up the rise to the front overlooking the lake. Carrie could only hurry along on her chubby little legs and my mom's "run" had more to do with pumping her arm, opposite to the one that was holding Carrie's hand, than actual fast movement. But they would do it. Slowly they would make it around the lake-side of the house and then down the gentle slope on the left-side of the house. To this day, I can still hear their laughter, and that little voice imploring, "Go round, Grandma, go round?"

That was the last good summer we had together. Mom's cancer continued to plague her and in the spring of the next year, she died. However, she lived more than twice as long as the doctors had predicted, and she was triumphant each day of the end of her life. The gift of cancer, is of course the chance… the time… to say goodbye. Mom fought this terrible disease with all her strength, but she also acknowledged that if her time on this earth were short, she would use it well. She loved us all, enjoyed the ups and downs in our lives, and without preaching left us with a sterling example of how to live a life full of love and face death with grace and without fear.

The Elephant's Trunk

By Garron Staten

For the leader of my herd, my wife Cecilia,
and my little parade of elephants, Lorelai and Trinity.
I am the stubborn rhino who you helped put on the right path.

Separated from their herds, a lone rhino and elephant desperately try to find their way back. Affected by the natural disaster that has separated them from their herds, one of them tries to make the best of the situation while the other allows his frustration to show through.

"Your nose is rather big," said the rhino to the elephant. "It's not like my horn that I use to scare away others."

"It's large," said the elephant, "but that is because I hold so many things inside."

The rhino slowly walked on careless of the elephant's remark. "What could you possibly hold inside your trunk but air?" he asked.

The elephant said nothing, but drew in water from the watering hole in which he stood. He sprayed the water into the sky and it rained down onto himself and the rhinoceros. "It's a rainmaker," he said. "It's my hose to take a shower."

The rhino shook his head in disbelief and charged toward the elephant who picked up a large log with his trunk.

"It's an arm," he said as he threw the log into the rhinoceros's path, stopping him in his tracks.

As the elephant walked away, the rhino who was foraging for food gnawed on grass. The elephant reached high for berries on a tree, picking them one by one.

"They're fingers," he said of the two protrusions on his trunk that he used to gently remove the berries.

The rhino wandered back to the watering hole to drink because the grass left him thirsty. The elephant came behind and slurped up water into his trunk. Placing the trunk inside his mouth, he let the water fall down his throat.

"It's a straw," he chuckled as the rhinoceros wrestled through the mud to get a drink.

The two journeyed onward through the hot African sun. They slowly trudged through the bushes and across the African plain. The sun got hotter and hotter and the insects bothered them. The elephant took sand into his trunk and with a blow, covered himself in a cloud of dust.

"Sunscreen and insect repellant," the elephant joked as sweat dripped from the rhino's skin and he used his tail to swat away flies.

The two kept on walking as the sun beamed down.

"I hope we find a watering hole soon. I'm thirsty," whined the rhino.

"My trunk is also a shovel," explained the elephant. "I'll dig you up some water."

The rhino laughed sarcastically, but before he stopped the elephant had used his trunk to burrow deep into the sand at the edge of the savannah. Water bubbled up through the sand. The rhino gasped and waddled over to drink.

"Hmmph," he sounded as he walked off.

"We are close to the herds," the elephant told the rhino who was some distance ahead of him.

"I see nothing. How could you know how close we are?" the rhino argued.

"If you must know," said the elephant, "my trunk is an extra ear. I can hear the vibrations of the walking herd through the ground."

"I don't believe you. I won't fall for your tricks," responded the rhino as he walked faster.

"You don't believe me?" asked the elephant. "Listen," he said as he sounded a great thundering roar through the jungle. "It's also a trumpet," he told the rhino, "that I use to communicate with others like me."

Just then, echoes of similar sounds rang through the trees. The rhino stopped as a parade of smaller elephants connected trunk to tail cleared a path through the brush. In the clearing stood dozens of elephants drinking from a pool of water. The elephant with the drive to thrive made it to his destination through determination. The rhino dropped his head, but he raised it when he heard rhinoceroses bathing in the pool as well. He hurried over to them and joined the herd knowing that he couldn't have gotten here on his own.

"Look at those trunks!" the other rhinoceroses teased the elephant herd.

"Wait until you see what's inside," said the rhinoceros with a very knowing smile.

Naomi

By Alexandra Kinias

Her innocence would be hard to prove, for nobody would believe that she had stabbed him in self-defense. Still in a state of shock with her heart pounding inside her chest Naomi sat in the back seat of the cab with her feverish two-year-old daughter, Zahara, in her lap, drowning in fear and panic. Her future was at stake. Six months ago she escaped from the refugee camp, crossed the Sudanese desert and illegally crossed the borders into Egypt. She almost died of hunger and thirst in order to save herself from an imminent fate if had she stayed behind. The risks she took were not for herself, but to offer her daughter a better life than the painful one she had endured. How fate had sabotaged her dreams and hopes in a blink of an eye and left her a fugitive running away from her present. The drunken loser lived off his rich and famous wife who was well connected to powerful people, and it would be hard for Naomi to run away forever from the police.

When she was offered the job as a housekeeper in the lavish residence of the movie star, she thought her troubles would temporarily diminish, but the drunken young husband wouldn't leave her alone. And that night he was totally wasted. The traces of the white powder he sniffed were all over the desk he sat behind in the den when her misfortune walked her inside the room. She tried to run away, but he grabbed her forcefully by the arm, threw her body on the desk and pushed himself on top of her. She fought hard, but he wouldn't let go. Naomi reached for the letter opener and stabbed him in the chest. She didn't stop until she felt his thick hot blood covering her. She threw the letter opener from her hand and ran away leaving her finger prints all over.

Recollection of the details of this incident made her shiver and she looked over her shoulder. The streets were crowded. Her sad hazel eyes scanned the mass congestion in the street. The four intersecting Cairo streets were jam-packed with cars. Five rows of cars drove in three-lane streets and brought the traffic to a complete halt. Loud nerve-wracking horns blew nonstop and her temples were on the verge of exploding. Pedestrians crowded the sidewalks and spilled over into the streets. Traffic police officers stood in the intersections. They blew their whistles for the cars to move, but the streets were uncontrolled. She was lost in the crowd and for a moment she felt safe.

Zahara's ear infection made her restless. The painkiller that Naomi gave her earlier together with the antibiotic hadn't taken effect yet. The heat and the noise drove the poor little girl over the edge. She squealed in pain and as she lifted her hand to touch her ear; she dropped her worn-out stuffed bunny to the cab floor. Naomi reached for it, held the girl close to her heart and softly bounced her fragile body up and down on her knees.

The cab driver lit a cigarette and exhaled the smoke inside the cab. It blended with the exhaust smell from the cars' mufflers and made Naomi dizzy. It was getting late; the street lights were glowing as well as the neon lights from the shops on both sides of the street. As the traffic slowed down, she could hear the loud music echoing from inside the surrounding cars. She was already late and worrisome thoughts that Mousa and the others would leave her behind filled her mind. He warned her not to be late. She cracked her knuckles and waited impatiently for the traffic to move. The idea of them leaving her behind scared her. She twirled her long cornrow braids and wondered how a single moment three hours ago had changed her fate.

After crossing the borders illegally into Egypt, she had applied for a refugee status and then applied for asylum in America, where her brother had also sought refuge when he escaped their doomed lands. Her refugee status was being processed for her repatriation with her brother, and under no circumstances the thought of fleeing the country would have crossed her mind. But now she was cornered, like a mouse in a trap, with no other option left for her. Her only salvation was to cross the Egyptian desert into Israel with Mousa and the other Sudanese refugees, a place where their immediate prospect looked brighter.

Father Alissio had opened the gates of his church to all the Sudanese refugees and Naomi found shelter there when she arrived to Cairo, exhausted and penniless. She met Mousa for the first time in the church's courtyard. It was the day of the Christmas market. The refugees were selling handcrafts and small gifts to the church goers, to supplement the meager allowance they received from the High Commissioner of Refugees [HCR]. On that day Mousa had just been notified that his refugee status was suspended. He was angry and frustrated with himself, with her and with the world. And when the photographer insisted to take a picture of him and Naomi, he forced a smile and then walked away. She never saw this photograph and when she asked the photographer days later, after all photos were finished, he told her that it was never developed.

Within the gates of the church Naomi and Mousa often crossed paths. He helped Father Alissio with work around the yard or he taught the Sudanese refugee children reading and writing in the only classroom. Other than casual greetings, they hardly exchanged any conversation and because of that Naomi was perplexed at his hostile behavior towards her. But for some strange reason she knew all along that she could trust him. A few hours earlier when she sought his help, Mousa insisted that she should flee the country with them. He confirmed her fears that she would get arrested for the crime she had committed and that her daughter would be thrown into an orphanage. Naomi couldn't bear the idea of losing yet another child.

Traffic moved slowly and the cab drove down an unpaved road in a slum neighborhood with wooden shacks on both sides. He stopped a distance from a warehouse. Naomi and Zahara got out. She looked around, but saw no familiar faces, and her heart swelled with panic and fear.

Among the crowds Naomi saw Mousa limping up and down the street with his backpack slinging over his shoulder. He stopped at the other intersection and his eyes scanned around. She approached him and he sighed in relief when he saw her.

"This is not the time to be late. Everybody is waiting for you. I was worried that they would insist on leaving without you."

His soft firm voice sounded in her ears like the most beautiful melody she had ever heard and she was overwhelmed with relief.

She wanted to explain to him that it was not her fault, but he didn't give her a chance. He walked away and she followed him in silence to the warehouse. On the way she saw women gathered around a water pump washing their clothes, in the streetlight. Laundry hung on ropes to dry in every window. Loud music blared from a kiosk that sold cigarettes and juice. Stray cats gathered around the garbage in front of the buildings and hissed at each other.

Some kids played soccer, others chased goats and chickens, rolled car tires and ran after them, and straddled wooden sticks and trotted around. Naomi was appalled to see her son Hazma run after a chicken. She called his name, but he ignored her and ran away with the kids. She hurried after him and grabbed him by the arm.

"Where do you think you're going?" she scolded.

Naomi

The little boy looked up at her. She stared at him in disbelief and felt a lump in her throat as she realized that he was not her son. Haunting images from her village flashed in front of her eyes. She witnessed the Janjaweed Militia on horseback raid the village in Darfur. She envisioned them shooting at her little boy in front of her eyes, and she glimpsed herself weeping and wailing as he died between her arms. She saw them burning down the village, stealing the cattle and raping the women.

Naomi's eyes brimmed with burning tears and her vision got blurry. Mousa noticed what had just happened, but didn't say a word. He took Zahara from her and entered the warehouse. Naomi followed them.

Inside the warehouse, other refugees were waiting impatiently. A young boy had crossed his arms on a table, rested his head on them and slept. His pregnant mother slept in a chair and her head tilted on her chest. Her husband was glancing at a black and white television screen that played an American action movie. He held a rosary in his hand and twirled its beads around his fingers.

A red truck was parked on the other side of the warehouse. Two men sat in the corner and smoked water-pipes. The smoke swirling from the burnt tobacco flooded the air with apple scent. Hay stacks covered the grounds and the walls of the warehouse. The whirling fan in the ceiling blew the loose hay around the old car tires that crammed the place. Three young Sudanese men rested their backs against the tires and sat in silence.

At the sight of Naomi, the husband woke up his wife and his boy, and the three young men jumped off the ground. They all grabbed their meager belongings and waited as the Egyptian men whispered among themselves. One man walked to the car and started the engine while the other waved at the Sudanese.

"Let's go. Get on."

The husband climbed on the truck's back and helped his pregnant wife and his son to get on. Mousa helped Naomi and Zahara. The three young men climbed in last.

"We are driving for three hours to the check point. When we arrive, none of you are to make a sound under any condition or else we're in trouble," the driver said in a firm commanding voice and then looked at the women. "And make sure the kids don't make any noise."

The pregnant woman nodded. Naomi cleared her throat. "My little girl needs some medication in an hour."

"I don't care. Give it to her now. We are not stopping for any reason."

Naomi opened the bottle of antibiotic and gave her daughter a spoonful of the red sweet syrup.

"Now you all lay down."

They lay flat in the back of the truck that was covered with hay, old blankets and burlap sacks. The two men buried them under heaps of straw, got into the car, started the engine and drove out of the warehouse.

The heat, noise, the hustle and bustle, and road pits made the ride uncomfortable. The bodies of the people in the back of the truck were tossed back and forth. After what seemed like eternity the noise and light of the city faded. The road became smoother and the vehicle gained speed.

Zahara twisted about, restless in her mother's arms.

The truck drove to the border city of Rafaah. The hay protected the refugees from the night chills, but its odor was unpleasant to inhale. After two and a half hours on the road, the driver slowed down as he approached the police check point and the bodies of the refugees were temporarily relieved from bouncing and shaking in their uncomfortable positions. At the check point, soldiers with machine guns sat in two police trucks parked on each side of the road, which was blocked with old rusty metal barrels.

***

An officer inspected the papers of a truck loaded with vegetable and fruit boxes. Another officer sat behind a small table on the side of the road, sipped tea from a glass and watched. The vegetable truck driver got out and opened the back and a soldier climbed on, opened a box, checked its contents and with a long stick he poked the bottom under the fruit and vegetable boxes. The soldier gave the officer thumbs up and jumped off. The driver got back behind the wheel. The officer handed him back his papers and banged on the truck's roof.

"Move it. Get going."

The soldier removed the two rusty barrels off the road, allowed the vegetable truck to pass through and then blocked the road with the barrels again.

The driver of the red truck inhaled deeply from the cigarette he held between his fingers and pulled over behind the barrels. The officer peeked through the car window to inspect the driver who kept his composure, but avoided looking the officer in the eyes. The other man in the passenger's seat looked out of his window.

"Papers."

The driver opened the glove compartment and handed the officer the car registration papers and offered him a cigarette from the box on the dashboard. The officer declined by ignoring the driver and thoroughly inspected the papers, in the silver beam reflecting from the street light. He frowned as he read and then looked at the driver who was already fidgeting in his seat. They exchanged a long glance.

"Where are you going?"

"Rafaah."

The officer handed him back the papers and then stuck his head deep inside the car and eyed a stack of hundred pound bills in the glove compartment and gestured at them with his chin. Quickly the driver got the money out and tucked it into the officer's shirt pocket. The officer backed his head out of the truck's window and banged on its roof.

"Get going."

The soldier removed the two barrels and the truck passed through.

They drove away on the asphalt road and by night fall reached a dirt road surrounded by barren sand and craggy mountains. The truck bumped and straw fell off. The driver saw light at a distance and drove towards it. He approached a wooden hut in the middle of nowhere with a light bulb dangling on the outside wall and two Land Cruisers parked in front. One of the Land Cruisers was packed with more Sudanese refugees. Four Bedouin men with scarves covering their heads and most of their faces sat crossed legged on the ground in front of a fire pit and drank tea. The driver of the red truck stopped the engine and got out. The Bedouins got off the ground, helped him remove the hay from over the refugees, and directed them into the back of the other Land Cruiser. Two Bedouins got into each car and they drove away leaving the red truck behind.

***

Naomi lost track of time and dozed off in the back of the car with Zahara and her stuffed bunny in her arms. When she woke up the sun was already crawling back in the sky, announcing the birth of a new day. The engines of the Land Cruisers roared in the arid desert that was surrounded by a sea of sand where nothing was visible but the horizon.

Suddenly a sandstorm blustered. The wailing wind hissed and howled as it stirred clouds with fine grains of sand that covered the sun. Visibility was diminishing by the second and in no time, a thick curtain of dust descended from the sky, covered the horizon and visibility totally vanished. Trapped in this desolate desert, the concerned refugees huddled in the back of the Cruisers. The eyes in their tired faces were filled with fear. The women hugged the scared children and the older couples cuddled under blankets. As they waited in anticipation for the dust storm to settle, darkness dropped over the sand. The delay was unexpected. It made them all anxious and it showed on their faces, but in this sand storm the drivers could not challenge their fate. They opened the backs of the trucks, allowed the refugees to get off and informed them that they would wait until the storm settled. It was a good opportunity to stretch her body and to give Zahara her medication.

The following morning the sandstorm died as suddenly as it had started and the visibility allowed the drivers to resume the trip. The drivers, their partners and the young Sudanese men dug the Cruisers out from under the sand where they were almost buried. They drove away among endless sand dunes with head lights on and kept a short distance between them. They crossed high sand ridges that led to sharp descents. The driver of the leading Cruiser scanned the desert with hawk eyes while the second one tailgated him in silence. Their two partners next to them pointed their machine guns out of the windows in anticipation of any sudden raid from the border patrol.

After endless hours of driving across the vast sea of sand, the cars stopped in the middle of nowhere. The sun was already setting and the Bedouins asked the refugees to get off and to wait until it got dark. When darkness fell they resumed their journey, this time in darkness. Not to be spotted by the border police, the two Cruisers drove with no headlights on, and stopped a mile and a half away from the border. The fatigued, hungry and thirsty refugees got out of the cars and walked in the darkness with two of the Bedouin men who were armed with their machine guns. The drivers waited behind for their partners to return. There was no moon in the sky, but it had cleared after the sandstorm and millions of stars sparkled above their heads.

One guide pointed straight ahead. "You are going to cross at border marker number six across from Beer Sheva."

They looked to where he had pointed and at a distance they saw light in the window of a rusted Egyptian watchtower that was resting on top of a ridge on the high edge along the mountain.

The refugees looked at each other and then at the guide in confusion. He had pointed to the border checkpoint.

"You can't just cross from anywhere you want. Yes it's dangerous to go over there, but you have to cross where there are people on the other side. You want to make sure to be found by the Israelis or else you will die in the desert." The impatient guide explained.

It was a decisive moment for the refugees, but they had paid their sweat and blood to get to this point and there was no going back. They walked in silence with the guides towards a crack in the ridge. From below, they saw the border on top of the ridge covered with rocks and a stretch of wire fence, in front of barbwire. Through a dirty window they saw the shadows of the border guards moving inside the watchtower.

The guide looked at his watch. "Wait until they change shift at midnight. That's about half an hour from now. And make sure not to make any sound. They are all armed and ready to shoot at anything that they see moving."

The guides turned and walked away and soon their silhouettes disappeared in the darkness of the night like ghosts. The refugees walked in silence toward the border and nothing was heard but the sound of their breaths. Even Zahara was quiet.

Mousa gazed at the sparkling stars above. Naomi remembered that she overheard him telling Father Alissio one night when he was working late that clear nights remind him of his childhood when he spent the summers in his grandparents' village in Darfur and slept in the yard under the stars listening to the crickets. And how this peaceful image of stars inspired him to become a writer. He explained to Father Alissio that he wrote about everything his government didn't like to hear about. He was arrested and his legs were broken in torture chambers. They threatened to break his fingers too if he didn't stop writing. And when he couldn't write anymore, he fled the country seeking a better life, but he ended up jobless with no future.

Naomi hoped that he would put all that behind him. In less than a mile he would be inside the Promised Land where his future would definitely be brighter.

Finally, they were at the border. One at a time, they crawled through a small opening between the barbwire and the ground. The men crawled in and the women handed them the children. Mousa, Naomi and Zahara were at the end of the line. Mousa crawled through the barbwire, crossed under the fence and entered the other side of the border. He looked at the sky and sighed in relief. He waited for Naomi to hand him Zahara, but a sudden cry from the little girl pierced the night. The Sudanese who were already inside the fence ran deep into Israel. Then, they heard the Egyptian border guards shout and flood lights illuminated the darkness. From the watchtower, Naomi saw them raising their weapons.

A border guard shouted in a loud speaker, "Stop. Don't move."

Naomi froze, took Zahara between her arms and ducked down. Mousa limped back to the barbwire and yelled at her. "Come on, get in."

The border guards opened fire at him and he fell to the ground. His blood splattered around and smudged his backpack.

Border guards approached Naomi, grabbed her by the arm and dragged her to the Border Patrol truck. With no resistance, she walked along in shock as Zahara's screams echoed around. Two guards with machine guns escorted her to the truck. She climbed into its back and vanished in its darkness. The two armed guards followed her in. She sat between them in total disbelief. She clutched to her daughter and hummed a sad melody in a low voice. The truck drove away from the barbwire. Naomi looked back and saw the stuffed bunny on the ground before the flood lights went off.

She was lost in her thoughts until the rusty creaking sound of a metal door brought her back to reality. The officer forcefully pushed her inside the dark empty cell. She lost her balance and almost tumbled to the ground with Zahara, but her body hit the dirty wall and that stopped her fall. The officer closed the cell door. She inhaled the damp air that smelled of mold and held tighter to her daughter. She rested her back against the wall, squatted and then sat on the floor. In her blurry mind she remembered hearing the officer mentioning something about transporting her back to Cairo for trial.

She bit her lips and closed her eyes. She sighed in anguish as she thought about her son. She wished that in her sleep she would dream about him just one more time. She couldn't salvage a photo of him when her village was burned down and she was fearful that she would eventually forget how he looked. She wanted to hold him, to touch him, to tell him how much she missed him and how much she loved him. All she wished for was just a dream, but even sleep was unattainable. Tears rolled down her eyes and she brushed them off with her hand.

Naomi was wide awake when the sun crept lazily into the cell from a small window in the ceiling. Zahara was sound asleep when the cell door opened and a guard yelled at her. She walked out and guards with machine guns escorted her and three other handcuffed prisoners to a police truck parked in the courtyard. Naomi carried Zahara in one hand and in the other hand she had Mousa's backpack that the officer gave her. It was stained with blood and had a bullet hole in it.

The truck wobbled on the road to Cairo. Naomi opened Mousa's backpack and looked inside it. In the dim light that came through a small slit covered with metal bars at the back of the truck she saw Mousa's English-Arabic dictionary. She pulled it out. It had a bullet hole in it.

She flipped through the pages and a photograph fell out. She picked it up and lifted it towards a ray of light. It was their photograph that was taken in the church courtyard the first day they met at the Christmas market. It was damaged and its edges were burned, probably from the bullet. She remembered that both of them had a grim expression on their faces and the photographer had asked them to smile to the camera. They both forced a smile. She gazed at the photograph and bit her lips. Her vision got blurry. Her eyes were filled with tears. She put back the photograph between the pages of the dictionary and tucked it back inside the backpack. She couldn't believe that Mousa had feelings for her, but kept them from her.

The prison truck rattled and bounced on its way back to Cairo. Its metal body was absorbing the hot sunrays and it raised the temperature inside. The prisoners were getting uncomfortable and Zahara moaned in pain as her medications were wearing out. In her despair, Naomi sang her a soft melody to calm her down, but the girl wouldn't stop fidgeting or whining. Naomi didn't blame her; she was just sorry for bringing her into a world of pain and injustice. For Naomi, it seemed that she had accomplished nothing but cross the African Sahara from one end to the other, always running away in hope of finding a place she can settle and call home, but to no avail. She didn't care anymore about herself or her life, but she knew that the next battle would be for her daughter. No matter what happened, she wouldn't allow them to take her daughter away. She had to find a way to send Zahara to her brother in America to raise her up and give her an education and hope to live.

The truck stopped and as the latch clanked, Naomi's heart fell to the ground. That was the end of her journey. The door opened and she followed the other prisoners out. She squinted in the glaring sunlight, held to the rail with one hand and stepped down from the truck while carrying Zahara over her shoulder. A woman approached her and tried to take Zahara off her shoulder, but Naomi pushed her away forcefully.

"Hey. Naomi. It's me. I am here to help you."

Naomi opened her eyes wide and saw Marylyn Baroln from the HCR office that was helping her with her refugee status. Standing next to her was a middle aged man in a suit and tie. Marylyn tried again to carry Zahara off Naomi's shoulder, but Naomi growled at her.

"No one is taking my daughter away."

"No one is taking her away from you. Relax."

Reluctantly Naomi handed Zahara to Marylyn.

"Oh dear! The girl is boiling with fever."

Naomi looked at the man in suit and tie as if she had just noticed him. Marylyn introduced him as a lawyer.

"What were you thinking? Trying to run away and crossing the border."

"I had to. Now it is all over."

"My dear girl, nothing is over. You have your whole life ahead of you. Yes, you are facing charges, but murder is not one of them. Luckily, the man you stabbed didn't die. The primary investigator concluded that it was self-defense. Our lawyer will make sure that you will stay the minimum amount of time in custody."

Naomi slapped her face with her palms and cried. "No one is going to take my daughter away from me."

"No one is taking your girl from you. Zahara can stay with you while you are in custody until she stops breastfeeding. And meanwhile, we will issue a permit to bring your brother over here to get her. I promise you."

Naomi's heart swelled with happiness and relief. If this was not a miracle, she didn't know what else could be....

To Say Goodbye

By Ellen Gibbons

Weak and withered flesh comes upon us.
We try to hold fast and be strong,
But we cannot.
Cascading veils abound.
Sometimes they are welcomed.
Sometimes they are not.
That last quiet breath.
The icy touch of flesh.
The desire to cover with a warm blanket
as if this would bring them comfort.
To say goodbye is only the beginning.
We will learn to say hello once again
and be comforted in the sweet density
of memory and love.

Renewal

By Anna Wilder

Often my life has not gone as planned. Chronic illness dissipated my hopes and dreams. Then when I dared hope again, new health problems crushed me. But once I worked through the grieving and anger, I found times of renewal. A greater appreciation for what I grew, new life rose from the ashes, and a sense of childlike wonder returned.

In the movie, *It's A Wonderful Life*, George Bailey kept losing one expectation and one dream after another. His dreams of travelling, having an important job, prestige, and money all dissipated over the years. His darkest moment came when it looked like his savings and loan business was going to be lost. However, an angel showed him how many lives he changed by his acts of kindness and love. At the end, he ran through the streets shouting and rejoicing as he realized the wonder of the life he had built.

In the 1980s, I went through a depression and a major illness. I struggled with the loss of the ability to work or go to school more than part time. Dreams of having a school degree, a career, or a family seemed far away. Finally, health returned. That summer, while working at a camp, I experienced a wonderful sense of renewal and hope. Spending time with my friends was a delight. The mountains around me stood tall and strong. The singing of a bird, the rushing of a stream, the green of the trees, the sparrow hawks wheeling overhead were all new and more beautiful than I could remember. I stood one day and cried tears of joy. The ability to work seemed more precious than ever, because I knew what it was like not to be able to reach for my dreams.

In Disney's *Fantasia 2000*, there was a beautiful story of renewal set to the music of Stravinsky's *Firebird Suite*. It started out with an elk walking through a forest covered in winter snow. The elk awakened his friend the sprite from an icicle. Gladly spreading spring across the land, the sprite made flowers and trees bloom. But when she got to the volcano, she couldn't turn it green.

The volcano erupted, destroying everything in its path. Trees were left blackened and charred. Gray ashes fell slowly to the ground. The elk found the sprite buried in ashes. It nudged her, but she crouched in dejection. It seemed a dark moment, but then the elk tenderly lifted her with its antlers. As it ran with the sprite riding, tears coursed down her face and dropped to the ground. Where the tears fell, green plants sprang up. When the sprite saw this, she was heartened. Joyfully she sent rain across the land. Flying across the forest, she turned everything green again. In the end, she even covered the volcano with green and life.

I came to Arizona with dreams of building a new life for myself. I had been through enough winters; it was time for spring. But when once again my health failed steadily, and I watched my dreams shatter one by one, I was so angry and hurt. I lost my job, and everyday tasks such as making meals and cleaning became increasingly difficult. My blood sugar and heart wouldn't work right, and soon I couldn't even stand without collapsing. Wondering what I had done to deserve a whole new illness, I felt buried under the ashes of my dreams and expectations. How could I dare hope again when there was such a chance of loss?

Finally, under my tears, I began to see the formation of new hopes. I found meaning in inspiring movies and books. Returning to school gave me new perspectives. Learning of different cultures and disabilities helped me see how others have coped with the struggles of life. Gaining computer skills opened up possibilities. Only in letting go of old expectations have I dared to plant the seeds of new dreams.

Because I spent so long in the dark, childlike wonder and laughter have become priceless gifts. In the movie *Hook*, Peter Pan had left Neverland and grown up. As a corporate lawyer, his business was more important to him than spending time with his children. When his children were kidnapped, he returned to Neverland to find them. In order to help them, he had to remember what it was like to be a child. To learn to fly again, he learned to think of a happy thought. By regaining a child's imagination, he learned to be Peter Pan again and to defeat Hook. Once back in London, when his business partner called him, he tossed the phone out the window and hugged his family.

One summer, I went with my friend to the lake, and we built a sand castle and splashed and played in the water. Another time, my husband and I walked along a lake shore and enjoyed feeling the sand between our toes. Trying to chase a motorboat, my dog got several feet out across the water before he sank. He was so excited that he forgot that he couldn't walk on water.

This last year, after five years of inability, my husband and I went with my parents to Las Vegas. We had fun at *Star Trek: The Experience*. We thoroughly enjoyed being beamed up to the Enterprise, and taking a wild ride in a space shuttle. The next day, we went to the Excalibur, where they had a jousting tournament. We got to see the knights of King Arthur's court battle with the evil wizard and dragons.

Simple things, such as laughter, everyday life, spending time with loved ones, and being able to get up and do things I used to take for granted, seemed so much more precious after losing them for a time. I learned that life could be wonderful, even when it didn't turn out as planned, and that hope could spring up from the ashes of old expectations. When it seemed like the light would never return, I remembered the Psalm (30:5) that says, "weeping may endure for a night, but joy cometh in the morning."

Homespun Philosophy

By Anna Laurene Arnett

Experience has given me insight to gradually
spin a philosophy, which I'll explain.
Since I come from Deity, Father has love for me,
angels watch over me, growth to sustain.
Then all things that come to me, sickness — vitality,
failure — prosperity, pleasure — or pain,
come either deservedly, through toil — or laxity,
else they are good for me, so why complain?

In this world of sin and woe, it seems where e're I go,
troubled winds always blow, hedging my way.
If that's what I'm looking for, tragedies by the score,
crowding forevermore, darken my day.
But when I am earnestly seeking the praiseworthy,
speaking up cheerfully, my sorrows wane.
When I keep my attitude reflecting gratitude,
I reach new altitude and peace obtain.

Drive to Thrive

The trick is to:
like what I have to do, gladly, my work pursue,
pause often to review strengths in my course.
Convert each stumbling block into foundation rock,
with courage meet each knock what e'er the source.
Just learning from negative, enjoying positive
is a prerogative I can employ.
When I use tenacity, I find capacity
and the audacity to claim pure joy.

Grow Where You Are Planted

By Martha Petronella Larsen van der Wal

I was married in Hilversum, The Netherlands to the love of my life, Niels Brannick Larsen, who was born in Morenci, Arizona. We met while Niels was serving a mission for The Church of Jesus Christ of Latter-day Saints in Holland. When the United States Army sent him back overseas to West Germany he used his leave to visit and then court me.

We first moved to Mannheim, Germany into a very small apartment, with a kitchen and bathroom that we shared with our German landlady's family. That in itself was a challenge in as much as I was married in the year 1954, only nine years after a bitter war had ended. I was Dutch and my feelings toward Germans had not yet out grown the "you are my enemy stage." My husband was an American and was occupying the country of my former enemy and was my hero-liberator. That combination was not a good ground for making friends with my neighbors where Americans were barely tolerated and Holland was remembered as a cold wet country. The Dutch were remembered for causing constant trouble by sabotaging the German Reich as much as possible.

I was taught by my very dear and patriotic parents: "Grow where you are planted and make things better than they were." With that philosophy I went forth with hope in my heart and mustered the courage each day to live life to the best of my ability. I could speak the German language, taught to me in school, and was somewhat familiar with the culture where I landed rather against my expectations. I spoke English with my American friends and my husband, although in our home we also spoke my native Dutch language a lot.

What a challenge it was to learn to master an American cook book with American measurements and try to produce an American pie, which I had never seen, or tasted, with my German landlady looking over my shoulders trying to put in some friendly advice. Needless to say, when the thing came out of the oven—by the way I had cooked it in an angel food cake pan, because I did not know what a pie pan was—my husband to whom I proudly showed my afternoon effort did not recognize what it was.

Niels said, "What is this?"

My feelings were hurt. "It is an apple pie."

He laughed. "Really?" He took me for a short drive to the American PX and we went to the bakery where I found out what a real pie was.

While in Germany I gave birth to my daughter Margaret and 14 months later, my son Brannick. That was a real experience for me. Giving birth normally is difficult in itself, but getting directions during the process of labor and delivery from the doctor in German and from the nurse in English, neither one my native language, made the process even more difficult. I had purchased a pocket size English/Dutch dictionary and took it to the hospital with me, in fact I took it everywhere— shopping, church etc. Still, I occasionally came home with the wrong thing. However not so with the babies, I figured out what was expected of me and did well.

Niels' tour in Germany drew to a close. Right after Christmas 1956, I left with my children on the train to Holland and my husband moved into the Army barracks while we were gone. It was hard to say goodbye to my brother and sister and their families, but I was comforted that my widowed mother would accompany us to America.

When we left Germany for the United States, our baby was 2 months and my little girl was 18 months. We left Bremershaven on a troop ship.

It should have taken us one week to New York Harbor, but we were hit by a storm—one of the worst the captain had ever experienced. And so it took us two whole days longer. The baby became very ill and so did my little girl and my husband. Personally I did not get seasick at all. My mother travelled with us and she was very sick also. I was never so glad to see the Statue of Liberty and land in general. We were intending to visit New York City, but we were all so worn out that we booked a flight to Tucson, Arizona to meet my husband's parents who lived in Bisbee, Arizona at that time.

We arrived late on a Saturday night and were picked up by my husband's parents and drove on to Bisbee. That was the first time I met my in-laws.

The house was very different than what I was used to. The food was different, and at first I was so tired of hearing English and trying to translate not only everything I heard but also everything I wanted to say. I still thought in Dutch and had to speak English. Though I was bound and determined to make this work, it was far from easy. My mother's inspiration: "grow where you are planted" was constantly in my mind. Since Mother spoke very little English herself, I translated for her.

My baby was still not doing well and when I checked his weight on Sunday he had lost three pounds on the boat. Thank goodness he was eleven pounds when he was born. Now he barely weighed eight pounds. Worst of all he did not act right. He did not cry and was very listless. I felt I had to find a doctor. On Monday my mother-in-law found a doctor that would take me in Douglas, Arizona. My mother-in-law taught school, I did not drive very well and my mother did not drive at all. We made it over there with help of my father-in-law. Thanks to my dictionary, I found out Brannick had double pneumonia and on top of that had been fed the wrong formula on board ship.

It took us several weeks to get that little boy healthy enough to travel from Arizona to my husband's new assignment in Ford Meade, Maryland, which meant travelling five days by car, resting every night in a motel, which again I had never before heard of. We bought a car, a Studebaker, and rented a U-Haul trailer to take some furniture and other helpful things to set up housekeeping in Severn, Maryland. Most of those items were given to us by family members who wanted to help out.

In Germany, our household goods were packed by the Army while I was in Holland saying goodbye to my family. When our things arrived in the middle January of 1957 at the house we rented we were curious why there was such an oversized crate among our things. We could not remember having anything that size, except for an armchair that had belonged to my grandmother—but it was not in a closed crate. We opened the tall crate first and laughed and laughed. The army in its ambitious, helpful attitude had shipped our Christmas tree, with all the ornaments and trim still on it. The tree had lost all its needles some of the decorations had fallen off and were broken on the bottom of the crate - they were glass in those days. It was really quite hilarious.

I found out that mail from home was delivered to a mailbox at the end of the road, about a mile walk from our house. If I wanted to send some mail out I had to put up the red flag, and the mail man was kind enough to pick it up. I was anxious for the mail that took three weeks by air and six weeks by boat to arrive. My mother had flown back to Holland from Washington, DC. She and my sister and brother were faithful writers. I did not want to wait until my husband came home at five o'clock in the evening so I went upstairs, to a storage area with a window. From there you could see the end of the road and the mailbox—

the object of my anxiety. I took my husband's binoculars and started to watch for the mailman at different times with the question in mind what time he came, and if he put something in it? After several tries and some trips with no success I did find that 10:30 was the usual time. I took up my post and watched at the right time and when something had been put in I took the babies and we went for a walk. Well sometimes I found what I wished for, sometimes bills only, sometimes advertisements and sometimes even a package from Oma far away and sometimes a package from Grandma in Arizona. I even eventually met the mail man and we became friends. He thought it funny he was watched through binoculars; but it had worked for me. "Grow where you are planted," even when the methods are sometimes very unorthodox.

My English was improving steadily, but my dictionary was still my friend, especially at doctor visits and in stores.

Being in the army caused us to move around quite often. Our next assignment was in California at Camp Irwin in the middle of the desert. The challenge there was desert heat, scorpions and tarantulas—I did not know spiders would get that big—and of course snakes. Holland does not have any of those things. Our trailer park was at the edge of the desert with no fence. You walked a few yards and you were in the desert. One morning my little girl was playing with a little neighbor girl. It was in the fall and the heat was bearable. She had a little red woolen cap with a white pom-pom on top that she had insisted on wearing that morning and they were playing in our back yard. When I did not hear them laugh and giggle anymore, I looked out of the window and they were gone from the spot they had just been. My husband was out on maneuvers and was not to be home for another week. I had no friends yet. What was I to do? I picked up my little boy and walked out into the desert— which I learned later was not smart to do—hunting frantically. Nothing. Everything looked the same, or so it seemed. I was crying.

By then Brannick was walking while I held his hand tightly. I was taught to pray and did so each morning and evening with my family regularly. I stopped and knelt down on the sand, put my arm around my boy and prayed to my Heavenly Father for help to find my little girl and that she would be unharmed. I got up off my knees and took off looking again. In a matter of minutes I saw something red in the distance. I walked as quickly as I could and I called her name. There she was in a little gully. I was beyond any happiness I had ever felt. I thanked my Father in Heaven first for his help and we all walked home to our trailer. We then got in our car, which I could now drive, and went into Barstow and we bought ice cream cones. I also never objected to her wearing her red woolen cap anymore—no matter how hot it was.

Not long after that my husband received orders to go to Korea for 13 months and we could not accompany him. My husband moved our trailer to Bisbee, Arizona and parked it on his parents' property where my father-in-law was a Phelps Dodge mine superintendent. After my little boy's second birthday in November, my husband left us for what seemed forever at that time. Although I was with family, I barely knew them, and I felt lonely. I was home sick for Holland and felt almost abandoned. It was a very difficult 13 months. Thank goodness for faith, for children that kept me very busy and letters from both sides of the world. Niels had a saying he used often. It said, "This too shall pass." And of course it did and again I "grew where I was planted."

He came home safely, for which we were grateful. We were together once more and decided that we did not ever want to be separated again. After thirteen years in the army, he did not renew his enlistment. Instead, we went to Flagstaff, Arizona and we went back to college. I earned my bachelor degree in elementary education and Niels graduated with a master's degree in education.

We did wonderful things together, we raised six children of our own and fostered several more. Niels and I taught school side-by-side. We fulfilled a mission for our church and struggled with illness, which ultimately took his life. Through it all we kept the faith and held fast to "this too shall pass." By encouraging each other, we managed to grow where we were planted and always had the drive to thrive.

My Town

By J. Ray Hendricks

I live in a small town…

If you've ever driven through my town, you probably didn't notice it. I don't mind that you didn't notice. Just to look at, as you drive 75 mph down I-40 through Arizona, there isn't much to see. We are one of those, "If you blinked, you missed it," kind of towns. If you have a minute though, I would like to tell you about my town.

My town has a population of around 1,400, barely enough to fill a section at a large stadium. Washington, DC politicians don't spend any money in my town, nor do they much care how their policies, passed in large "houses", affect us here in our small houses.

Speaking of homes, in my town the neighbor with the two-story house leans over the fence for an afternoon conversation with his neighbor in the single-wide mobile home. There isn't a zoning commission in my town that separates its citizens into classes. There are no homeowners associations, no yard police, and whether you're rich or poor you have at least one broken-down vehicle on your property.

My town isn't perfect, I will tell you that right now. Anybody who lives here has offended someone, been offended, or both. In some regards we are no different than any other place you might live. We have our share of scandals, there's a drug dealer or two, and a good story can get passed quicker than the blame for an embassy attack.

Like any family, we have our quarrels and spats, but we also know how to celebrate. Homecoming, The Fourth of July, Halloween, and others are lauded each year. The young men post over 20 flags down Main Street, and in almost every yard on holidays. At Christmas time the teenagers crowd onto trailers loaded with hay bales and sing carols over the chug-a-lug of the tractor as they make their way through town. On Christmas Eve much of the town meets at the far end of Main Street. Working together they set out luminaries from one end of town to the other, their soft glow warming hearts, and a cold winter street, in celebration of the birth of the Christ Child. Cups of hot chocolate afterward warm the frozen hands but even the propane heaters can't unthaw the smiles.

My favorite celebration each year is Founder's Day. It's a celebration of the founding of the city in 1876. Many of those who have moved away make the trek each year bringing their families back to enjoy the festivities. There is a parade, where among all the other floats, you can see a motorized bed complete with the Smiths in full 1950's night dress. You can try the 5k run, eat a pancake breakfast, or enjoy reenactments at the park. All of the wannabe Michael Jordan's in town show up for the basketball tournament and the rodeo is always a kids favorite.

One of the favorites I became acquainted with was the firing of the anvil. Ivan, an old cowboy in town, has two anvils. One is mounted firmly on a trailer, the other is raised above it hoisted by a chain. He pours black powder onto the the bottom anvil and then drops the upper anvil onto the lower one and its waiting charge. The result is a cannon like blast which can be heard through the whole town. Ivan is notorious for two things.

1. He begins this Founder's Day morning ritual at about 4:30 am.

2. He is particularly fond of setting the first charges off in the drives of the newest folks in town.

I found out both of these things on my first Founder's Day. My wife, who was raised in this small town, failed to inform me of Ivan and his antics when we moved into town. I was peacefully asleep, awaiting a beautiful spring morning, when the windows of our single-wide trailer imploded with the concussion of what I was sure was the beginning of a war. Startled from sleep I was stopped mid-stride, loaded .44 in hand, by my wife. She said, "It's just Ivan and his anvil." I replied still disoriented and confused, "What the hell is an Ivan and what the hell is an anvil?"

For me though, the best part of Founder's Day is the dance. About eight o'clock that night music starts playing in the old elementary gym. From 90 years old to nine months old, friends and family fill the floor. There are lots of boots and white hats atop young, cowboy-hopefuls, as well as a few with some saggy pants in desperate need of belts.

If you were to come and spend the evening with us you would learn; a little two step, the cupid shuffle, the YMCA, and The Cotton Eyed Joe. You would also see a pair of five-year-old kids tentatively sharing their first dance to the mellow sounds of George Strait while a couple nearing their eighties might be sharing their last.

By the way, two thirds of the boys at that dance would have a knife clipped to their pocket and the same percentage of men would have a loaded gun in their boot or in the door pocket of their unlocked truck in the parking lot.

But if you really want to know about my town let me tell you a story. Recently there was a terrible accident in my town. Two boys on their way to football practice collided with a school bus. Both were badly injured. When word reached the rest of the team, dressed out on the football field, the high school boys in my town knelt down in prayer for their friends. That's my town.

The very next day, school was let out early so the student body could assemble for a picture. The students and faculty held signs saying, "Get well!" and "We love you!" The pictures were hurriedly framed and delivered to the boys awaiting surgeries at the hospital along with banners and footballs signed by the entire team and coaching staff. That's my town.

Realizing the financial burden of travel to hospitals over 80 miles away and the loss of work as well as other considerations, a few compassionate women quickly got together and began planning a day of fund raising. They held a Zumbathon, dinner, auction, raffle, and a dance. In one night they raised over $8000.00 for the two families. That's my town.

Any good town has a high school rival and we have ours. We boo and hiss and cheer each other in fierce competition at anything from parking spots to state championships. When word of the accident reached our rivals practicing on their football field, the Mogollon Mustangs of Heber Arizona took a knee and prayed for their fallen foes, now friends in need. They took up a collection and at the charity dance presented a check for over $250.00. Heber, I'm still going to cheer just as loudly for my home team and I expect you to do the same, but due to this selfless act of the good, young men in your town; you are welcome in mine.

As a matter of fact, anyone is welcome to come to my town. If you want to steal from me, the keys are probably in the ignition or above the visor, but you may have to outrun that .44 still under my pillow or my wife's .38 under hers. You'll find knives in pockets of our young men and hard work under their nails. You'll find young women who can still be total hotties and turn the boy's heads wearing clothes that leave more covered than bare. They also haven't forgotten how to bake grandma's chocolate chip cookies; but don't think about trying anything with them—cause most can out-shoot the boys. That's right you'll find us clinging to our God and our guns, but you'll also find us clinging to each other. So come on and we'll laugh together, we'll do some crying together, and then we'll dance, 'cause that's my town.

Pink

By Betsy Love

The elephant has to go. I place Tiny in the wagon next to the cow bank. After balancing the sailboat on the top of all my other treasures, I drag my radio flyer wagon out of the pink garage. Can you believe it—our whole house is pink. I don't know what my mother was thinking when she painted it that way. Dad said it was because that color was special to her. She has no idea how silly I feel living in a pink house.

I line up my toys along the driveway in the grass, their price tags showing. Last night Mom helped me decide on the prices. I might have enough for my PlayStation after today. All I need is ten more dollars.

Waiting for the first customers, I touch Tiny's chipped ear. I remember when Dad brought him home from his trip to India. It doesn't look much different than the ones you can buy in a toy store. But because Dad dragged him all the way back across the ocean makes him that much more special. I pick him up and hold him so I can see the details painted along his back, and flipping him over, I see where Dad carved my initials. I can't sell this one, he's too special. So I tuck him in a hiding place in the garage so he won't be sold.

Back at my place on the lawn, I notice the stuffed bear. Grandma gave it to me for Christmas when I was a baby. We used to live with her then because Daddy was going to school. I press my face into the matted fur and pretend I can smell her favorite perfume. Grandma sprayed it on its fur when we moved far away so I could remember her when I missed her. The smell is long gone, but I imagine lavender and mint. No, I can't sell this one either. I put him with the elephant.

I wait for customers. A nice lady with a little girl picks up the Mickey Mouse hat. My insides feel funny. Not my hat, I think. I bought that with my own money when we went to Disneyland three years ago. That's the year that Grandpa died. He used to make a squeaky mouse sound and tease me about my bug-eye glasses. He said they matched the ears on my hat. I snatch it. "I don't know how that got in there." I race it into the garage and hide it under the teddy bear.

The bully from the street wanders onto the driveway. His bike is parked next to the light pole. "Got any dollies?" He picks up the green car and makes varoom varoom noises and bumps it along the cement, before crashing it into the wheel of the wagon.

"That's not for sale!" I yank it from him, surprised that I had the guts to do so.

Mom looks up from her book. "Arnold, I think you best go on home now."

Arnold kicks at the wagon, the ray gun topples out, but I'm fast and snatch it up. I race it and the car into the garage and hide them with my other treasures.

My wagon is almost empty now. Just an old pair of goggles from when I learned how to swim at summer camp and the birdhouse I built in cub scouts. I can't sell those either. I spent too long painting the triangular piece of wood to house a nest. I'll hang it in the back yard and put some seed in it. No sense in wasting a masterpiece.

Last is my sailboat. Just before we moved a year ago, Mom and I sailed it one more time on the lake behind our house. I just can't get rid of this. I look over at Mom. She pulls her hat down over her bald head. I look back at the sailboat. It's the last time we'll ever get to do something like that again.

Dad brings out glasses of lemonade and hands a couple of pills to Mom. "How's the sale coming?" He asks.

"Great." She says. "Maybe we'll have enough to pay for that trip back to Seattle after all." That's where she is from, where Grandma still lives. Mom wants to go see her old home one more time before....

My eyes mist up and I drag the back of my hand over my nose. I'm supposed to be too young to understand what's happening. But I do.

I look at my empty wagon and then into the shadowed garage where my treasures are hidden, and then I steal a glance at Mom. Her eyes are tired from the treatments. I know what I have to do.

At the end of the day, I empty my cow bank. I look into Mom's eyes and hand her not only my PlayStation money, but what I made from selling my treasures. "Now you can go to Seattle."

Four Years of Joyful Service

By Margaret L. Turley

Niels sat in the cardiologist's office flanked by his wife and oldest daughter. The doctor looked up from the test results with a grim expression on his face. "Mr. Larsen, you have six months."

Niels looked at his daughter's shocked expression. His wife squeezed his hand.

"We need to start you on heart medication, place you on a strict diet, and send you home with oxygen." The doctor closed the chart. "Your heart is weak and enlarged, that is why you've been short of breath."

"But I exercise every day." Niels didn't understand. He lived an active life, and had recently accepted early retirement. Every day he hiked in the sandy wash lined with cottonwood trees and tamaracks with his cocker spaniel, D.O.G. He would circle back under the I-40 overpass and walk back through town, frequently visiting with friends along the way. His route worked into a five-mile jaunt. His plans didn't involve being stuck at home tied to an oxygen machine. He had six children and 18 grandchildren with lots of baseball and football games and other events to attend. He wanted to serve a mission with his wife and had dreams of riding cross-country on motorcycles with his sons.

He walked out of the doctor's office, depressed that the end of his teaching career was also the end of his life. On the trip home they stopped at the medical supply store for the oxygen he needed and the pharmacy for his medicine.

His wife, Martha, imposed restrictions on Niels' diet immediately. No more salt, fat or sugar. Eating used to be one of his pleasures. Now food was tasteless and boring. No more ice cream, bacon, or other favorites.

Between the medications and his heart condition, Niels felt weak and faint. He had difficulty walking from the bedroom to the living room. Martha learned how to measure Niels' blood pressure and pulse but didn't feel confident she could do anything correctly. Martha was nervous and sought assistance from their children and from friends in the community. Nothing made Niels feel well. He decided it would be better to die, in order to remove the burden and worry from his wife.

Six months passed. Niels was tired of sitting in his chair and waiting for fate to take its course. Eldon, his youngest son who lived close by came over to visit. "Hey Dad, I bought a trailer so we can haul the horses and go hunting."

"I'm tied down with a 200-foot leash with this oxygen." Niels yanked on the detested green tubing. He'd spliced several pieces together so that he could sit outside on the front porch and throw balls for D.O.G. to fetch. It bugged him that he couldn't even walk out the back door to feed and water his horses that nickered their greetings to him.

"Jan already has the permits for our favorite spot over by Alpine." Eldon ignored the hiss-pop, hiss-pop of the concentrator. "We bought a double-down sleeping bag and we'll put a mattress in the bed of the truck. With the shell you'll sleep nice and cozy."

"I'd like to go one more time." He never could hit the side of a barn, but that wasn't what the annual ritual was about. He loved nature. One of his favorite side jobs had been working for the forest service when he attended Northern Arizona University. He regretted that he wasn't able to take his family to man the watch tower that summer he started teaching in Winslow.

"It's been six months, I'm obviously still here. Let's go!" Niels was excited about relishing the crisp autumn air in the mountains on horseback with his sons. The oxygen equipment was returned to the vendor along the way. Tethers to medical accoutrements were slashed and he was determined to live each remaining moment to the fullest. He hoped the weakness didn't come back to haunt him like the gophers that plagued his fields and rerouted irrigation water to hither and yon with their holes.

They drove southeast from the dusty red Northern Arizona plateau dotted with shrubs to the mountain forests of pine and ash. Niels rode horses with his sons and reminisced about all the other times they'd gone out together. Sitting across the crackling campfire he marveled at how much his boys looked like carbon copies of his younger self with the same square teeth and dark hair. They even used the same mannerisms. On the way home he insisted on stopping at Dairy Queen for a large strawberry milkshake, six months of no ice cream was worse than a death sentence.

After returning home he felt so well that he talked to his wife, who had retired from teaching school about serving in the temple together. The trip to the temple was four hours one-way. So they decided to purchase a mobile home to stay at while in Mesa during the week and return home on the weekends. With new purpose, Niels drove down and back, while his wife read from scriptures and good books. He loved to read, and spent plenty a night finishing one more chapter; but he liked to listen to Martha read even more.

Though winter weather frequently caused road closures, their temple work days were never delayed or cancelled. In the temple where they were all dressed in white, Niels looked at his bride and felt young and vital once more. He felt that Heavenly Father was pleased with his service and blessed them with clear driving conditions on their scheduled travel days.

It was a year after receiving the six-month verdict. Niels felt strong and was happy to be active. While in Mesa, he walked every day, feeding the pigeons in Pioneer Park along the way. He and Martha would watch out for other animals. One particular favorite was a black and white collie who climbed to the roof of one of the houses on their route. He would woof his greeting as they walked by. When at home in Joseph City, he cheered at ball games where his son coached and grandchildren played and walked with his faithful companion, D.O.G.

Niels accepted a calling to lead music in Primary, the children's meeting at church. Music and singing was a favorite activity since he was young. He'd taken voice lessons while stationed in Germany. He sang and Martha accompanied him for many events, including weddings and funerals. He entertained his children and students with songs like "The Big Brown Bear Said Woof" and "Old Man River." Many evenings were spent at the piano, singing with his wife: "Somewhere in the West, We'll build a little nest, and let the rest of the world go by."

They had done just that. Niels and Martha had built their home in Joseph City. Niels had cleared several acres of land south of their house and planted big gardens every year. He built a barn and grew alfalfa so his children could learn about farming. They raised cows, pigs and chickens. Over the years, he added turkeys and geese, always had at least one horse and was never without a dog.

Now he was back to the profession he loved, teaching children music. His warm baritone voice blended with the primary children while singing: "I love to see the temple, I'm going there someday. . ."

At the two-year mark the cardiologist shook his head. "You are doing amazingly well. Keep on doing whatever you are doing."

Niels proudly stood his full five-foot nine-inches tall. He and Martha were ecstatic.

Then calamity hit. The annual monsoons came with a vengeance and caused a flood. The run off backed up from the railroad tracks where silt had built up over the years blocking the wash, through the fields he'd cleared from tamaracks and planted melons, corn and tons of vegetables that Martha bottled and stored, past the barn with last year's hay. Their home was in the direct path, after the muddy water passed through the town sewer ponds. In moments their house and most of their belongings were covered in murky sewage.

Friends and neighbors rushed in to rescue what could be dragged out and stored the items in Eldon's father-in-law's warehouse at no charge. Their son, Brannick helped set up pumps as soon as the water level dropped low enough to remove the water. There was little hope to salvage the remains. The putrid smell assured them the property would be condemned.

Niels' sister, Nelda loaned them her family fifth-wheel trailer to reside in, and a friend allowed them to park on their property with electricity, water and sewage access while they looked for a new place. They appreciated the accommodations, but frequently wondered where a particular item had ended up. Was it in Mesa, in storage, in the fifth-wheel or lost in the flood.

While they were in Mesa, Niels and Martha found a double-wide mobile home they reluctantly decided would serve as their new house. They signed the contract and scheduled delivery to Joseph City after they called and made arrangements with a friend for a lot to place it on.

When they returned home that weekend, their bishop called them to come into his office. "The Lord wants you to keep your home. Church and community members will rebuild it for you."

Niels sobbed. His frame shook. They were blessed yet again.

Once the original structure of their flooded property was pumped out, and fans blew it dry, volunteers gutted the house the Larsen family had lived in for over 30 years. The sheet rock and floors were hauled to the dump. The contaminated dirt was dug out from the foundation. Then everything was replaced from the subfloors on up. By winter they were back in their own home, completely refurbished with furniture and appliances from their daughter and other donations. Instead of having the usual green exterior the house had always been, it was now blue.

Throughout this entire process Niels and Martha continued to serve in the Mesa temple. He felt it was only a small part of what he could return for the blessings they had received. The mobile home was sold to a new family who moved to Joseph City. This relieved them of the financial burden, and left room to make new plans for the future.

They made an appointment to talk with the bishop.

"We want to serve a mission." Niels served his mission as a young man in The Netherlands. That is where he met and taught Martha and her mother, new converts to The Church of Jesus Christ of Latter-day Saints. "We want to go back to Holland as a couple."

"That is wonderful. Your health is improved, but it may not be wise to leave the continental states. You still have a bad heart." The bishop rubbed his chin. "I am sure there is a perfect spot the Lord has in mind for you."

They were thrilled when they received their calling to serve as temple missionaries in Washington, DC. It was a little less than three years since being diagnosed with cardiomyopathy when they packed their belongings and drove north to Provo, Utah to attend Missionary Training Center.

On the way to Utah, they stopped in Cortez, Colorado to visit with their daughter, Nella and her family. While they were there, Martha tripped and injured her foot, causing a laceration that almost severed her toe. Niels took her to the emergency room where she was stitched up.

The doctor looked Martha in the eye. "Diabetes and wounds are a dangerous combination. There's no such thing as a minor wound to the foot—even a small foot sore can turn into an ulcer that, if not properly treated, can lead to amputation."

Martha was discharged with crutches, a prescription for antibiotics and told to keep her foot elevated.

Niels was worried. "Do you want me to call headquarters and ask for a delay until your foot is healed?"

"No. Let's keep going."

They bid farewell to Nella and her family. Their car was stuffed to the brim with the necessities for housekeeping and suitcases, so Martha propped her bandaged foot on the dashboard rather than sitting with her legs propped up on the back seat.

They arrived in Provo in February 1999. The Mission president arranged for them to stay in a ground level home close to the temple in Salt Lake City for their two weeks of training. Then he made follow-up appointments with a doctor for Martha's foot. When it was time to transfer east to DC, Martha was still on crutches, and a huge snow storm was predicted. Their son Brannick called and volunteered to drive their car out to DC.

"We were worried about you driving across country with your heart and Sister Larsen's foot." The mission president sighed with relief. "We will fly you out, and fly your son back home after he delivers your car and belongings." He cleared his throat. "There is a single sister who was reluctant to fly alone. Now she will be in your excellent company."

"Thank you. This is an answer to prayer." Niels was comforted.

They were met at Dulles airport by their new Mission President and taken to their furnished apartment in Kensington. By the time Brannick arrived with the car a week later, Martha was walking without crutches. They were happy to have transportation and be able to explore. After getting settled, they felt Heavenly Father had sent them as close to Holland as possible without sending them overseas. The lush green foliage and humidity stood in stark contrast to their high desert home. There were many Dutch shops within walking distance and an outdoor market with flowers, fruit and vegetables grown by local farmers. Niels especially liked the bakery on the corner where they purchased fresh bread almost every day.

Niels and Martha loved serving in the Washington, DC temple. They enjoyed visiting national monuments, museums, the Library of Congress and traveling to historical sites in surrounding states. One of Niels' favorite subjects and minor in college was history. Here he had the chance to visit sites where many of those events occurred. They made numerous friends with other missionary couples. Family and friends from the US and from Holland visited them in their Kensington apartment where they were entertained by George, a squirrel that Niels fed peanuts. Several squirrels would come up on the balcony, grab a peanut and rush back to their tree. George had no fear. He would bravely nudge the screen door open and wander inside and follow his nose to the closet where they stored a 20-pound bag. He helped himself to the mother lode.

Niels continued his walks, relishing the nature trails that started in their backyard. Trees stretched their branches across the path, forming a shady canopy.

They had served for ten months when suddenly Niels had difficulty breathing and was admitted to the intensive care unit with double pneumonia. His weak heart failed.

The doctor patted Martha's hand. "You may want to call your children and let them know their father is going to die."

She could hardly get the words out between sobs as she called each of their children.

Amid Christmas rush traveling, all six of their sons and daughters left their families and jobs and flew to DC to see their father before he passed on to the next realm. Within 24 hours Margaret, Brannick, Jan, Nella, Eldon and Maria had gathered at his bedside.

More than a week slowly passed. Brilliant lights and cheery music defied the worry and sorrow the family waded through. The hours in the hospital waiting rooms were spent reminiscing about the wonderful things their father had done to support them such as Niels coaching a little league team. He accepted all the boys who wanted to play that had been rejected by other teams, including his sons. There was no place for them to practice, so Niels cleared tamaracks, plowed and leveled a field for them, and took them on to victory. He changed from refereeing football and basketball, to keeping score and driving the bus so he could be there for his own children.

Everyone had family and jobs they needed to return to. The oldest son, Brannick stayed behind to support Martha, the rest flew home. Niels battled the pneumonia, and hoped his heart would rally again.

The mission president went to the hospital to visit Niels.

"Would you like a blessing?"

Niels nodded weakly.

The president placed his hands on Niels' head and offered a special prayer. "The Lord will bless you to regain your strength and complete your mission."

Miraculously Niels began to heal. He was discharged from the hospital and celebrated Christmas in their new apartment with Martha and Brannick. Their church friends had moved them from the third floor down to the first so that Niels would not have to negotiate stairs. They felt extremely fortunate once more, almost four years past the time the first cardiologist had given a six-month life expectancy.

Martha continued to perform her regular temple duties while Brannick remained behind to care for Niels.

One morning Brannick woke to find his father fully dressed and ready to leave. "Where are you going?"

Niels' expression was calm. "I am going to the temple."

"I am coming with you." Brannick quickly dressed and drove Niels to the temple, then wheeled him inside so that he could attend a session.

Colleagues tapped Martha on her shoulder and told her it was great to see Niels back in the temple. Martha shook her head. She had left him at home in the care of their son. She was busy and continued with the task at hand. A little while later she looked down the hall as Niels rolled out of an ordinance room smiling ear to ear. To her, he was as handsome as the day they married over 45 years earlier. Her heart soared.

Their youngest daughter Maria moved to Kensington to assist, Brannick returned to his family in Utah. Niels persisted in going to the temple as often as possible and made steady progress until he was able to serve in his full capacity as a temple missionary once more. True to the promise given in the healing prayer by the mission president, Niels was able to complete his mission with his companion, sweetheart wife, Martha.

Their middle daughter, Nella flew out to DC when it was time to pack up and go home. Nella and Maria drove the car while Niels and Martha flew home. Their eldest child, Margaret and youngest son, Eldon, along with his family met them at the airport.

Eldon waved the Diamondback tickets he purchased as a welcome home gift. "Look where we're going!"

Niels put his arm around Eldon's shoulder. "I want to go to the Mesa Temple." He put the tickets back in his son's pocket. "Mom and I started our temple service there and now we are home we want to go back."

Margaret arranged for a babysitter while she, Eldon and his wife Carol attended the temple with Niels and Martha. After the temple session, Eldon took his dad to the ball game, happy that his father was feeling well enough to do both.

One week later Niels felt ill. He had an appointment with a doctor in Flagstaff to get prescriptions for his heart medications. Martha hoped that the doctor would figure out what the problem was and get things back on track. Unfortunately, the doctor was inattentive, wrote out the prescriptions and told Niels to come back in three months. When they arrived home in Joseph City, Niels was too weak to walk. Their son, Eldon had to come and carry his father inside. Niels was tired and wanted to lie down in his own bed. Concerned family and friends convinced Martha that Niels needed to go back to the hospital emergency room, 70 miles away. When they arrived, the physician found it hard to believe that the doctor who had seen Niels earlier that day had sent him home. He admitted Niels to the hospital with pneumonia and heart failure—the lethal duo that had plagued him before.

Though Niels lay sick in the hospital, he didn't stop planning to give Temple service. He told Martha they needed to buy a cell phone so they would have more security on their trips up and down the Mogollon Rim to serve in the Mesa Temple again.

Martha refused to leave Niels alone in the hospital. Days stretched into weeks. Joseph City was too far away. Niels' sister, Nelda came to the rescue and paid for a hotel room for Martha and the rest of the family who came and took turns staying with Niels at his bedside. Even though he couldn't speak because of the breathing tube, he still communicated with his eternal companion with smiles and inside jokes.

On the 27th of September, 2000, 53 months after being diagnosed with severe end-stage cardiomyopathy Niels' heart beat its last time while he was surrounded by his wife, both his sisters, and his children.

More information about LDS temples can be found at:

http://www.lds.org/church/temples/why-we-build-temples?lang=eng
http://www.lds.org/general-conference/2011/04/the-holy-temple-a-beacon-to-the-world

About Writers Unite to Fight Cancer (WUFC)

Writers Unite to Fight Cancer (WUFC) was founded in June of 2010. Our mission is to increase community awareness about cancer and raise money for cancer research.

The money we raise supports both local and national cancer research programs, and is occasionally donated to cancer patients to assist in obtaining the care they need.

Authors who would like to join Writers Unite to Fight Cancer should contact Margaret at:

Margaret L. Turley, Administrator

1146 N. Mesa Dr. #102-233

Mesa, AZ 85201

Or Email: writersunitetofightcancer@gmail.com

More information can be found on the WUFC website:

writersunitetofightcancer.org

About the individual authors in this anthology:

Information about each author can be found on the WUFC Website under the "About" tab, in the author category in the drop-down menu. Authors are listed in alphabetical order by first name.